Let's Take the Kids to

London

fifth edition

DAVID STEWART WHITE
and
DEB HOSEY WHITE

ROARING FORTIES
P R E S S

Berkeley, California

Roaring Forties Press
1053 Santa Fe Avenue
Berkeley, CA 94706
www.roaringfortiespress.com

ISBNs:
978-1-938901-37-9 (Printed book)
978-1-938901-48-5 (ePub)
978-1-938901-47-8 (Kindle)
978-1-938901-46-1 (PDF)

For more information about family travel to London, please visit the book's website at www.KidsToLondon.com.

Although the authors and Roaring Forties Press have taken all reasonable care in preparing this book, we make no warranty about the accuracy or completeness of its content, and, to the maximum amount permitted, disclaim all liability arising from its use.

"London is so vast and varied, so rich in what is interesting, that to one who would wander among its treasures, it can be difficult to decide where to begin, and even more difficult to decide where to end. Indeed, to a book on London—to a thousand books on London—there is no end."

—*A Wander in London*, by E. V. Lucas

"Would you like an adventure now, or would you like to have your tea first?"

—*Peter Pan*, by J. M Barrie

Contents

Part 3 — Let's Take a Field Trip!

Part 4 — Stop Dreaming, Start Planning

Part 5 — Did You Forget Anything?

Acknowledgments

Our thanks to the many people on both sides of the pond who have assisted us along the way to this fifth edition of *Let's Take the Kids to London*. A nod to our children, Dan and Laura, whose travel adventures and encouragement helped launch this book.

Many thanks to Deirdre Greene and Nigel Quinney at Roaring Forties Press, who chose to publish the latest editions.

Introduction

London loves kids

L ondon is one of the world's most family friendly cities. With open arms, it welcomes kids to explore and make their own memories. Look around London and you notice children of all ages playing in parks, romping through fantastic playgrounds, skipping along the Thames Path to ride the London Eye, investigating hands-on museums, and soaking up history as they explore famous landmarks. The landscape of London invites children to look, listen, laugh, and learn.

London loves kids. You'll know it's true when you see a yeoman warder at the Tower of London bending down to listen to a child's question. Or you watch a teenaged tourist trying to elicit a smile from a stone-faced palace guard. Or you notice a museum guide quietly leading a child to the front of the group for the best view.

London and kids are made for each other. Having a little prince in the royal family isn't the only reason London is kid-centric these days. The city has long been the adopted home of Paddington Bear, and Peter Pan moved into Kensington Gardens ages ago. Harry Potter and his friends have been catching the train to Hogwarts from King's Cross Station for quite a few years now. Long ago, Mary Poppins landed in town and worked as a nanny. And Christopher Robin first met a bear named Pooh in the London Zoo before moving to the Hundred Acre Wood.

This latest edition of *Let's Take the Kids to London* includes updated information on the city's enduring tourist attractions and new descriptions of sites and activities for families traveling to London. It was carefully developed and correct when it was published. But a wise traveler checks local conditions before each trip. Some change is nearly constant—opening hours and admission prices change almost as quickly as London's fickle weather. And some change is almost negligible—the Ceremony of the Keys at the Tower of London has remained virtually unaltered for hundreds of years.

The Practical and the Poetic

Many travel books put the practical before the poetic. They describe what to pack, where to stay, and when to go before enumerating all the wonderful things to see and do at your destination. We've decided to flip-flop the order of the traditional travel book:

- First, learn something about London's family activities and its fantastic palaces, parks, theaters, cathedrals, and museums—the things you want to see and do.

- Then, browse through an extensive section on planning, where to stay, and other tips we have learned after many trips to London with kids.

There is a reason why the title of this book is *Let's Take the Kids to London.* That's exactly what we said when our family of four took its first, serendipitous trip to Britain. From that experience, the trips that followed, and many years of additional research, we converted the phrase into this book.

How to Read This Book

Read this book first with a cup of tea, feet propped up, kids in another room. Initial planning for a trip is a time for dreaming. We will paint a picture of London; you can imagine your family in the picture. As imagination turns to serious consideration, you'll need details on London's tourist attractions and activities. Feature boxes throughout the book will let you know:

- Where each place is located

- How to get there (usually by the Underground, or "Tube," London's subway)

- The exact street address
- Phone numbers and email addresses for more information
- Hours the site is open
- About how much time you can expect to spend at the site
- Admission cost ranges
- A website address

A little more about how this book is organized. It starts with the prime tourist destinations in central London. After that, it explores up and down the River Thames. Next, the book covers family activities in and around London. Then, we provide some ideas for field trips to give you a taste of what lies outside London in the English countryside. Finally, it's down to practical matters, with some planning advice and travel tips we have learned along the way.

Photographs

Our thanks to the organizations and individuals whose photographs are used in this edition. The copyright information for photos appears at the end of the book.

Central London West

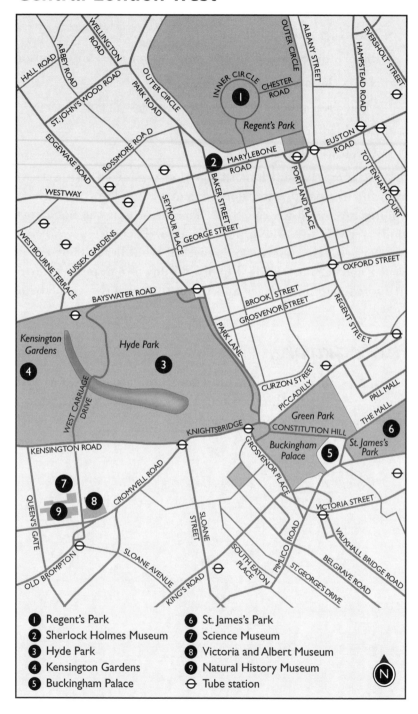

1. Regent's Park
2. Sherlock Holmes Museum
3. Hyde Park
4. Kensington Gardens
5. Buckingham Palace
6. St. James's Park
7. Science Museum
8. Victoria and Albert Museum
9. Natural History Museum
⊖ Tube station

Central London East

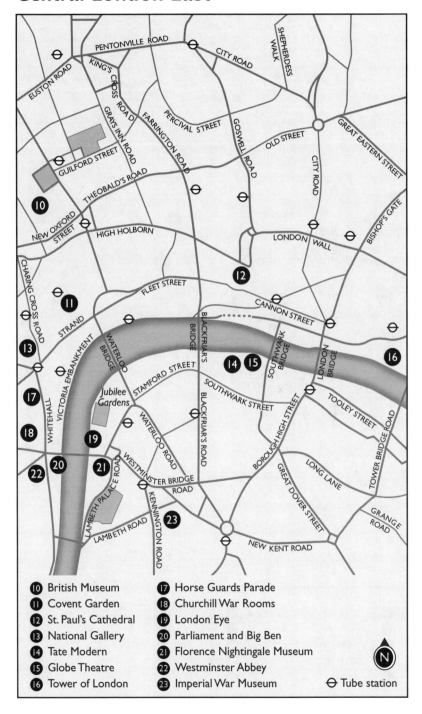

10 British Museum
11 Covent Garden
12 St. Paul's Cathedral
13 National Gallery
14 Tate Modern
15 Globe Theatre
16 Tower of London
17 Horse Guards Parade
18 Churchill War Rooms
19 London Eye
20 Parliament and Big Ben
21 Florence Nightingale Museum
22 Westminster Abbey
23 Imperial War Museum

⊖ Tube station

London Environs

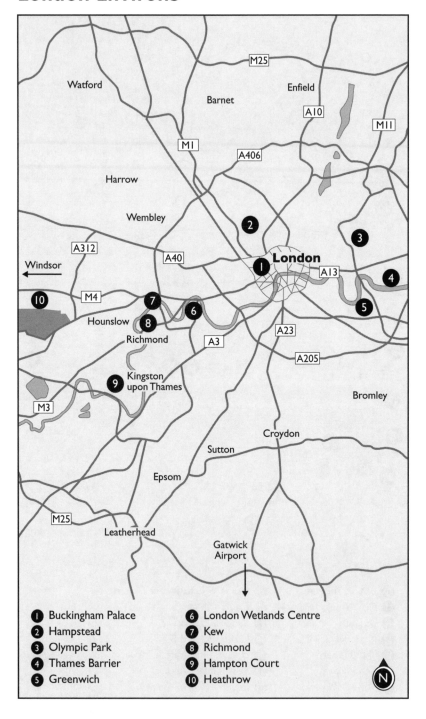

1 Buckingham Palace
2 Hampstead
3 Olympic Park
4 Thames Barrier
5 Greenwich
6 London Wetlands Centre
7 Kew
8 Richmond
9 Hampton Court
10 Heathrow

PART ONE

Look Kids! It's...

Towers and Bridges
Palaces and Horses
Old Dead Guys
Big Wigs
Flowers and Buskers
War and Peace
Museums — Some Serious, Some Not
An Art Museum or Two
Fun, but Perhaps a Tad Tacky
On the River

Towers and Bridges

Much of London's history is locked behind the imposing walls of the Tower of London. William Wallace, Anne Boleyn, Thomas Cromwell, and Catherine Howard were all temporary Tower residents. And, unlike the unfortunate prisoners who left the Tower without their heads, today's visitors can walk out the gates and tour another nearby landmark—the Tower Bridge.

The Tower of London

"I know where we're going," said Judy, as they turned a corner.

"It's the Tower of London!" exclaimed Jonathan.

Paddington had never been to the Tower of London before and he was most impressed. It was much, much bigger than he had pictured.

— *Paddington at the Tower*, by Michael Bond and Fred Banbery

Will kids enjoy the Tower of London? Absolutely! In fact, if you have time to take your children to only one historic spot in London, make it the Tower. The Tower of London offers a virtual smorgasbord of English history and culture within its ancient walls. Take your pick from this partial menu:

- Beauty—the crown jewels
- Tragedy—dismal dungeons and prison cells galore
- Legend—captive ravens and wandering ghosts
- Horror—beheadings on Tower Green
- Tradition—the ancient Ceremony of the Keys

The Tower's tour guides—yeoman warders—are informative and friendly, and most make a special effort to pique the interests of young visitors. A tour with a yeoman warder may be the "crown jewel" of a Tower visit because the warders provide an insider's perspective that is every bit as memorable as the real crown jewels displayed in the Tower.

Please don't call them beefeaters; these are yeoman warders, retired career members of the British military. The Tower of London is home to many of the thirty-seven warders who live with their families on the grounds. Look closely and you may spot the domestic mixed in with the historic—children's play equipment, a pet cat, hanging laundry, and other evidence of the residents' private lives. The Tower forms a walled village within the city of London, but the private pub and staff housing are not on the public tour.

One stop on the Tower tour where visitors may get a sense of the community is the Chapel of St. Peter ad Vincula. Although this is a royal chapel and historic site, it is also the local church for Tower residents. The royal family worships here on occasion, and this is also where yeoman warders' grandchildren may be baptized.

William the Conqueror began building the Tower in 1078, shortly after taking over England—his way of letting the natives know that London was under new management. The Tower was expanded over hundreds of years to become the fortress you see today. It has served as prison, palace, zoo, armory, execution spot, place of worship, and tourist attraction.

As a tourist destination, one of the Tower's most popular exhibits is the crown jewels. The exhibition was revamped in 2012 for the Diamond Jubilee of Queen Elizabeth II. The jewels are beautifully displayed, and although the lines to see them may be long, they are managed well. A moving walkway inches visitors past the jewel cases to ensure that no one lingers too long, but you can usually circle back for another look.

Children may find the security precautions in the Jewel House to be almost as impressive as the jewels themselves. The massive doors leave no doubt that you are walking through a very large vault to view the jewels. The high-tech, high-security Jewel House is a far cry from the original display of jewels in the Tower. In the seventeenth century, the crown jewels were simply locked in a cabinet. When visitors wanted to see the jewels, they just asked a custodian and paid a small fee! Not surprisingly, someone attempted to steal the jewels, but the thieves were caught making their getaway. Security was tightened, repeatedly, and the jewels have been safely guarded ever since.

The White Tower contains displays of ancient armor and weapons, including Tudor and Stuart royal armor, weapons from the reign of Henry VIII, and British war trophies. Kids will be drawn to the child-sized armor worn by young princes and to the equine armor that protected royal horses.

Tower Green was the site of several notorious executions. King Henry VIII had a frequent-chopper account here. Two of his wives—Anne Boleyn and Catherine Howard—were executed on the green after being imprisoned in the Tower. Queen Jane Grey was also beheaded in the Tower; all three unfortunate ladies are buried in the Chapel of St. Peter ad Vincula.

But for all its association with beheadings and imprisonment, the Tower today does not feel very macabre. Leave that to the London Dungeon or Madame Tussaud's Wax Museum. The Tower's yeoman warders may spin a few sinister stories of Tower executions that elicit "eews" and "yucks" from the audience, but the warders are so good-natured that a visit to the Tower is appropriate for all ages.

Sir Walter Raleigh was one famous Tower prisoner familiar to many American visitors. Imprisoned here three times, Sir Walter made himself quite comfortable in the Tower. His family moved in with him and brought along furniture, books, and other comforts of home. But—and this is a big "but"—Sir Walter was executed after his third stay in the Tower. He lost his head elsewhere in London, however, not on Tower Green.

Today the Tower's only prisoners are a flock of birds. Visitors will undoubtedly hear the legend: if the ravens leave the Tower of London, the town is toast! Actually, that's not exactly the legend, but it does explain why the birds' wings are clipped. The legend really says that if the ravens leave, the White Tower will crumble and disaster will befall England.

The national importance of the ravens was demonstrated during an unfortunate incident at the Tower of London. In preparation for a visit by the royal family, a police dog sniffed through the Tower grounds searching for possible bombs. Charlie the bomb dog was pecked by Charlie the raven. A former bird-hunter, canine Charlie grabbed raven Charlie in his mouth. The raven struggled and the dog instinctively bit down, killing the bird. The British press had a field day, members of the public were outraged, and the dog was demoted. But the yeoman warder who told us most of this story was nonplussed: "Not a big deal; we can always get another raven."

Canine threats are an ongoing concern for the yeoman warder responsible for the birds. The Tower's Raven Master locks the ravens into protective cages each night, in part because of London's burgeoning urban fox population.

During the summer months, thousands of tourists stream into the Tower of London. Plan to arrive as soon as it opens and head straight for the crown jewels to avoid the long lines found later in the day. You can buy a ticket in advance on the Tower's website, in a few London Underground stations, and from some tour operators.

The Tower of London

The Ceremony of the Keys

Want to see a free and nearly private ceremony in the Tower of London? The Tower allows about fifty people to attend the nightly Ceremony of the Keys—the ancient ceremonial locking of the Tower gates. Attending the ceremony requires advance planning. Tickets may be ordered from the Tower's website (search under "Ceremony of the Keys"). Tickets are free, except for a small administrative fee. You can obtain up to six tickets per booking from April through October; in other months, the limit is twelve tickets. Tickets are popular, so book as far in advance as possible. Photo identification is required when entering the ceremony, and children under eighteen must be accompanied by an adult.

On the night of the ceremony, ticket holders are escorted into the Tower at 9:30 p.m., long after other visitors have left. A yeoman warder explains the history of the solemn seven-hundred-year-old ceremonial locking of the Tower's gates. After a brief introduction, visitors line up near the Bloody Tower gate to watch the Tower of London's very real military guard unit escort the chief warder as he locks the Tower. Today, the Ceremony of the Keys is largely symbolic, but to understand how important this ceremony is, consider our family's experience.

A huge celebration was taking place at nearby Tower Bridge, a band was playing outside the Tower of London's walls, but arrangements had been made to stop the music during the Ceremony of the Keys, which had been going on every night for hundreds of years without interruption. Visitors gathered inside the Tower at the appointed hour. The guards were ready to begin the ceremony, but the band outside kept playing. The yeoman warder looked at his watch, frowned, and looked again—but still there was no break in the music. At this point the warder's supervisor appeared, barked a command into the microphone on his radio, and made a pointed comment about "putting an end to this nonsense." He ran off; a minute or so later, the band abruptly stopped midsong. Maybe it was coincidence, or maybe the bandleader was reminded of the many executions carried out just a few hundred feet away. In any case, the Ceremony of the Keys began.

On another visit to the Tower of London, we learned that not just the yeoman warders take the ceremony seriously. Different British military units rotate guard duty at the Tower. On this visit, the guards were Gurkhas, elite British Army troops from Nepal. During the ceremony, the guards' commands were issued in crisp, loud, and heavily accented English. It was the same ceremony as performed by regular British troops, but visitors almost needed subtitles to understand it. After the ceremony, a yeoman warder explained that the Gurkhas take guarding the Tower very seriously and very literally. The standing order for the guard is that all visitors have to leave the Tower immediately after attending the chapel service. One Christmas Eve, the Gurkha guards escorted everyone from the church out of the Tower—no exceptions—including family members of yeoman warders who lived on the grounds. The exiled family members had to phone friends at home inside the Tower to get back into their own homes! The Gurkha guards certainly secured the Tower, but you wonder if they allowed Santa in that night.

Here are a few practical hints for visitors attending the Ceremony of the Keys. Arrive early. If possible, stay in the front of the tour group, and stand directly opposite the gate to the Bloody Tower. When signaled by the yeoman warder, move quickly through the gate to see the completion of the ceremony in the inner courtyard. The yeoman warders ask that visitors not talk during the ceremony. Silence is more than a mark of respect: half the fun of the ceremony is listening to the sounds—the guards' synchronous footsteps on the cobblestones, the jangling keys, the shouted commands, the bugler's notes. One other important issue, especially for visitors with children, is that the Tower's restroom facilities are not open immediately before, during, or immediately after the Ceremony of the Keys. The following is a true story; the names have been omitted to protect the easily embarrassed.

Hearing the first footfalls of the guards, the father peered down the pathway toward the gate of the Byward Tower. "Dad. Dad!" whispered a small, urgent voice. "I have to go to the bathroom." Hoping against the inevitable, the father replied: "Can't you wait, son? The bathrooms are all closed." But alas, as every parent knows, when a child has to go, he *has* to go, even in the Tower of London. Fortunately, a sympathetic yeoman warder stepped in, earning the father's enduring gratitude. "Bring the little fellow this way," he offered, and led the pair through a gate toward the White Tower. "Let him use the wall; it's seen worse," said the ever-practical warder. The crisis was resolved, but the father missed the start of the ceremony. We have it on good authority that the father and the son returned to the Tower the following year to see the entire Ceremony of the Keys. This time, they planned ahead and used the public toilets at Tower Place just outside the Tower gates *before* the ceremony.

Tower Chapel Services and Special Events

Toilet emergencies aside, there is another way to see more of the Tower than the average tourist. If you are truly interested, ask a yeoman warder about attending church services in the Tower's Chapel Royal of St. Peter ad Vincula. Services are at 9:15 a.m. and 11:00 a.m. on most Sundays (no services in August). Remember, this is not a tourist event; it is a worship service for people who live in the Tower. Go with respect.

Special events abound at the Tower, especially on weekends in the summer, during school breaks, and around major holidays. It's a good idea to check the Historic Royal Palaces website for information on upcoming events. One event that is hard to ignore is a gun salute. For royal occasions, such as the monarch's birthday, a simple twenty-one-gun salute just won't do. The Tower fires off a sixty-two-gun salute: the traditional twenty-one-gun salute, plus twenty because the Tower is a royal palace and fortress, and twenty-one more as a mark of respect for the sovereign. Since the end of World War II, the Honourable Artillery Company, the oldest armed body in Britain, has fired gun salutes from four modern cannons on Tower Wharf.

An ambitious plan has improved landscaping, ticketing facilities, pedestrian walkways, river piers, and other areas in the neighborhood surrounding the Tower. With buildings and fortifications that are almost one thousand years old, archeological and restoration work is an ongoing endeavor at the Tower of London. Some of these projects unearth "new" information about the Tower's history, making the Tower more than a static historical site—it is living history.

WHERE? WHEN? £?

TOWER OF LONDON

Location: On the north bank of the Thames, downstream (east) of central London

Tube: Tower Hill station (Circle or District Line)

Address: Tower of London, Tower Hill, London EC3N 4AB

Phone: 0844 482 7777 (within UK); 020 3166 6000 (outside UK); telephone ticket sales: 0844 482 7799 (within UK)

Hours: March through October, the Tower is open from 9:00 a.m. to 5:30 p.m. Tuesday through Saturday. On Sunday and Monday, the hours are 10:00 a.m. to 5:30 p.m. The rest of the year, hours are 9:00 a.m. to 4:30 p.m. on Tuesday through Saturday and 10:00 a.m. to 4:30 p.m. on Sunday and Monday. Last admission is thirty minutes before closing. The Tower is closed December 24–26 and January 1. Yeoman warder tours operate every thirty minutes until 3:30 p.m. (2:30 in winter). These tours last about an hour.

Time needed: Three hours

Admission: Visiting the Tower of London is expensive but worthwhile. Discounts for families, students, and seniors may apply. If you plan to visit the Tower, Hampton Court, and at least one other Historic Royal Palaces property, consider purchasing an annual membership. Getting tickets in advance will let you avoid waiting in long lines. Buy tickets on the Tower's website, by telephone, from a London Underground Travel Information Centre, or at the Tower ticket office.

Facilities: New Armouries restaurant and Raven's snack kiosk inside Tower grounds, Apostrophe café and Perkin Reveller Restaurant on nearby wharf. Fast food and other options along Great Tower Street. No formal outdoor picnic areas, but visitors may bring food and sit on benches on the Tower's grounds. Toilets and baby-changing area in the restaurant and the Brick Tower. Many areas of the Tower are not wheelchair accessible.

Website: www.hrp.org.uk

Tower Bridge

Tower Bridge rivals Big Ben as the most recognizable landmark in London. Don't make the novice tourist's mistake of referring to Tower Bridge as London Bridge, its nondescript neighbor a mile upstream. Despite the famous children's song, London Bridge is a sturdy modern bridge in a historic location on the River Thames. Its predecessor was sold, dismantled, and reassembled as a tourist attraction in Lake Havasu, Arizona. Today's London Bridge is hardly a tourist attraction, but Tower Bridge deserves a visit.

Take a tour of the inner workings of the bridge and learn how the span was opened in Victorian times by huge steam engines. Kids can experiment with operating models and interactive computers that detail the drawbridge's engineering principles. Technically, Tower Bridge is a bascule bridge, from the French word for seesaw. Undoubtedly this is the largest seesaw in London. Once outside the engine rooms, take in the views from the top of the bridge, 140 feet above. Don't worry, this is an enclosed walkway, so nobody is going to fall off. The walkway was designed so that pedestrians could walk across even when the draw span was raised. But this required the visitor to detour up and down long stairways, and the walkway was closed not long after the bridge was built. The walkway was reopened in 1982 as part of the Tower Bridge Exhibition and has become a prime spot for viewing sights along the Thames.

If you want to forgo the museum and enclosed walkway, there is no charge to walk across the bridge itself. This is a prime spot to take a picture of the family, so set up the shot to include the Tower of London in the background. Lucky visitors may see the bridge being raised to let a ship go past. Bridge openings are rare these days because London is no longer the port that it once was. But there is no shortage of traffic *on* the bridge; nearly 150,000 cars, trucks, and buses cross this important London link every day.

Tower Bridge

WHERE? WHEN? £?

TOWER BRIDGE EXHIBITION

Location: Crosses the Thames at the Tower of London. Enter the exhibit and walkway on the northwest side of the bridge, closest to the Tower, through a glass-enclosed ticket booth and lobby.

Tube: London Bridge station (Northern or Jubilee Line) or Tower Hill station (Circle or District Line)

Address: The Tower Bridge Exhibition, Tower Bridge, London SE1 2UP

Phone/email: 020 7403 3761/ enquiries@towerbridge.org.uk

Hours: April through September, the exhibition is open from 10:00 a.m. to 6:00 p.m. October through March, the hours are 9:30 a.m. to 5:30 p.m. Last admission is thirty minutes before closing. Closed December 24–25.

Time needed: Sixty to ninety minutes

Admission: Ticket prices are moderate, and there are discounts for families, students, and seniors. Children under age five get in free. Tickets can be purchased at the bridge or online.

Facilities: Toilets and baby-changing areas. All areas are wheelchair accessible.

Website: www.towerbridge.org.uk

Palaces and Horses

R oyal residences, royal horses, and royal treasures are all parts of London's history. Although today's monarchy is mainly ceremonial, the trappings of royalty still serve important roles . . . as tourist attractions.

Buckingham Palace

> "By gumdrops!" whispered the Big Friendly Giant. "Is this really it?"
>
> "There's the Palace," Sophie whispered back.
>
> Not more than a hundred yards away, through the tall trees in the garden, across the mown lawn and the tidy flowerbeds, the massive shape of the Palace itself loomed through the darkness. It was made of whitish stone. The sheer size of it staggered the BFG.
>
> —*The BFG*, by Roald Dahl

The Big Friendly Giant had good reason to be impressed. A 2014 report on the world's most expensive houses ranked Buckingham Palace as number one, with a value of almost US $1.6 billion. The grandeur of Buckingham Palace comes not strictly from architecture but from its aura of tradition, ceremony, and power.

The royal family actually allows the public to peek inside Buckingham Palace. Just a peek, mind you, and only for a few weeks each year while the royals are on vacation. Under this arrangement, Buckingham Palace state rooms are usually open daily during August and September. Tourists are admitted at timed intervals, the lines can be long and security is tight. Audio tours are provided, including a family audio tour to help kids enjoy their visit.

Seeing the inside of Buckingham Palace is a novelty not only for foreign tourists. A fair number of British citizens take the tour to check out the inside of a place that has played an important, if ceremonial, role in their nation's history. During one August visit, we overheard a British mother telling her two daughters, "This is the piano where the young princesses Elizabeth and Margaret took their lessons when they were little girls." We will never know if this fact was impressive enough to inspire the visiting children to practice their lessons, but the mother deserves credit for trying. Another visiting child was unimpressed by the Buckingham Palace throne room: "That's the throne? It's just an old red chair!"

At the end of the Buckingham Place tour, visitors can stroll through parts of the palace's thirty-nine-acre private garden. A children's garden activity trail map is available. As the tour ends, there is an opportunity to browse the palace gift shop, filled with tasteful but expensive mementos of the visit.

The palace sometimes offers tours on select dates in December, January, and February. Complete with an end-of-tour glass of champagne and a ticket price to match, these guided tours are not geared to family groups. The rest of the year, tourists are reduced to gawking at Buckingham Palace through a tall iron fence. Invariably someone (usually a child) asks: "Is anybody home?" For an answer, take a look at the roof. If the royal standard—the flag with a lion on it—is flying, the monarch is in residence. Historically, no flag flew above the palace at other times, but now the British Union Jack flies at Buckingham when the royals are away from home.

By the way, when you peer through the fence, you're actually looking at the back of Buckingham Palace. The front of the palace overlooks the private gardens.

Buckingham Palace, viewed from St. James's Park

WHERE? WHEN? £?

BUCKINGHAM PALACE TOUR

Location: At the west end of the Mall, bordered by Hyde, Green, and St. James's Parks. Tours enter on the south side of the palace on Buckingham Palace Road and exit on Grosvenor Place.

Tube: Green Park station (Jubilee, Victoria, or Piccadilly Line), St. James's Park station (Circle or District Line), or Victoria station (Circle, District, or Victoria Line). Nearest tube stop at tour exit is Hyde Park Corner (Piccadilly Line).

Address: Ticket Sales and Information Office, The Official Residences of The Queen, London SW1A 1AA

Phone/email: 020 7766 7304/ bookinginfo@royalcollection.org.uk

Hours: The palace is generally open from late July (or early August) through September (or early October). Hours in July and August are usually 9:30 a.m. to 7:00 p.m. (last entry is 4:45 p.m.). September hours are usually 9:30 a.m. to 6:30 p.m. (last entry at 3:45 p.m.). Hours are subject to change.

Time needed: Two hours

Admission: Tickets to the palace are moderately expensive. There are discounts for families, students, and seniors, and children under age five get in free. Tickets can be ordered online or purchased at the ticket office, located on Buckingham Palace Road, on days when the palace is open. Ticket office opens at 9:30 a.m.

Facilities: Café in the palace's garden. Toilets are available at the end of the tour. Some areas of the palace are not wheelchair accessible. Strollers (push-chairs) and large packages must be checked at the entrance. Families may borrow baby carriers for use during the palace tour.

Websites: www.royal.gov.uk; www.royalcollection.org.uk

Several nearby tourist sites are associated with the palace:

- The Royal Mews
- Clarence House
- Wellington Arch
- The Queen's Gallery

For a slightly better peek into the royal backyard, especially the royal tennis courts, climb to the top of nearby Wellington Arch, once home to London's smallest police station. Climbing atop Wellington Arch and spying on the palace will entice many children, but the Queen's Gallery art collection and Clarence House may be of limited interest to kids. The Royal Mews, site of the palace's stables and carriage house, is another matter.

Horse Feathers? The Royal Mews

Why would a horse stable be called a mews? Originally, this was the home of the royal falcons, and mewing referred to the shedding of the birds' feathers. Today the Mews is the headquarters of the Crown Equerry—the motor pool for the royal family. (Doesn't "Crown Equerry" sound so much better than "motor pool"?) This is where the royal family's ceremonial coaches, limos, and horses are housed.

The royal family owns more than one hundred coaches and carriages; some of the most ornate are on display in the Royal Mews. For sheer opulence, check out the Gold State Coach. As the name implies, this coach is so heavily gilded, it's a wonder that the royal horses can even pull it. This golden fairy-tale coach has been used at every coronation since 1821. Slightly lower on the opulence scale is the Irish State Coach, used at the annual opening of Parliament, and the Glass Coach, which transported Lady Diana Spencer to St. Paul's Cathedral to begin her star-crossed marriage to Prince Charles.

For the 2011 wedding of Prince William to Kate Middleton, the newlyweds traveled from Westminster Abbey back to Buckingham Palace riding in a vintage carriage built in 1902 for the coronation of King Edward VII.

Children touring the Royal Mews may quickly conclude that once they've seen one golden coach, they've seen them all. Let's see the horses! Because the royal family lives in luxury at Buckingham Palace, it's hardly a surprise that the royal horses' quarters are none too shabby either. It doesn't even *smell* like a stable. The Cleveland Bay and Windsor Grey horses live in clean, bright stalls with tiled walls; each animal's name is displayed on a prominent placard.

The Royal Mews is also home to a fleet of automobiles. But the official in charge of the Mews has the title Master of the Queen's Horses, not Master of the Queen's Rolls-Royces, and it is horses and carriages that many tourists come to see. The Mews is an agreeable attraction for most children; for young equestrians, the Mews is a must-see.

Like the Tower of London, the Royal Mews is a historic site that serves as home to some of the people who work there. The Mews also features a learning room where kids can imagine, draw, and color their own royal carriages.

WHERE? WHEN? £?

THE ROYAL MEWS

Location: A few hundred yards south of the palace, where Buckingham Gate becomes Buckingham Palace Road

Tube: Victoria station (Circle, District, or Victoria Line)

Address: Ticket Sales and Information Office, The Official Residences of The Queen, London SW1A 1AA

Phone/email: 020 7766 7300/ bookinginfo@royalcollection.org.uk

Hours: In November and from February through March, the Mews is open Monday through Saturday from 10:00 a.m. to 4:00 p.m. From April through October it is open daily 10:00 a.m. to 5:00 p.m. Last admission is forty-five minutes before closing. Closed in December and January and periodically throughout the year for official events. Hours are subject to change.

Time needed: An hour (longer for horse lovers)

Admission: Tickets are reasonably priced, and there are discounts for families, students, and seniors. Children under age five get in free. Tickets can be ordered online or purchased at the Mews ticket office. Combination tickets for the Queen's Gallery are available.

Facilities: No food available on-site. Toilets and baby-changing areas. The site is wheelchair accessible.

Websites: www.royal.gov.uk; www.royalcollection.org.uk

Clarence House

No one lives forever, but before her death at age 101, Elizabeth, the Queen Mother, was truly pushing the longevity envelope. Clarence House was her home for almost half a century, from 1953 to 2002. Prince Charles moved into Clarence House and did a bit of redecorating after she died, but he kept much of the house the way his grandmother left it.

Clarence House was designed by John Nash, the same architect largely responsible for Buckingham Palace, Regent's Park, Marble Arch, and a host of other Regency-style structures in London. Clarence House was built in 1827, and the site was heavily damaged in World War II. Like Buckingham Palace, Clarence House is open to the public during the summer. Clarence

House is not a grand palace; the tour includes just a handful of official rooms on the ground floor of the building. There is little to interest children here, but the tour is relatively short.

WHERE? WHEN? £?

CLARENCE HOUSE

Location: A few hundred yards east of Buckingham Palace, along the Mall, opposite St. James's Park

Tube: Green Park station (Jubilee, Victoria, or Piccadilly Line)

Address: Clarence House, St. James's Palace, London SW1 1BA

Phone/email: 020 7766 7303/ bookinginfo@royalcollection.org.uk .

Hours: Open daily from 10:00 a.m. to 4:00 p.m. (5:30 p.m. on weekends) during the summer opening, generally in August and September. Last admission is one hour before closing.

Time needed: One hour

Admission: Tickets are reasonably priced, and there are discounts for children. Those under age five get in free. Tickets can be ordered online.

Facilities: No food or toilets available on-site. The site tour is wheelchair accessible. Strollers (pushchairs) and large packages must be checked at the entrance.

Websites: www.royal.gov.uk; www.royalcollection.org.uk

Wellington Arch

Wellington Arch

Except during the annual summer opening, the gates to Buckingham Palace are closed to the public. But tourists can sneak a peek of the palace grounds from Wellington Arch near Hyde Park Corner. Visitors can climb steps or take the elevator to the top of the arch and peer into the palace gardens and tennis courts.

Wellington Arch was built as to celebrate the victory of the Duke of Wellington over Napoleon Bonaparte. At one time, the arch sported a huge equestrian statue of the duke. That monstrosity was removed and the arch was relocated in the late 1800s. Now the arch supports the largest bronze sculpture in Europe— an angel of peace landing atop a horse-drawn chariot of war.

The arch was restored by the English Heritage preservation organization as part of Britain's millennium celebration and further renovated in 2012. English Heritage also operates nearby Apsley House, home of the Duke of Wellington.

WHERE? WHEN? £?

WELLINGTON ARCH

Location: Hyde Park Corner, between Hyde Park and Buckingham Palace

Tube: Hyde Park Corner station (Piccadilly Line)

Address: Apsley Way, Hyde Park Corner, London W1J 7JZ

Phone: 020 7930 2726

Hours: Open Wednesday through Sunday from 10:00 a.m. to 5:00 p.m. Closes at 4:00 p.m. November through March. Closed Good Friday, December 24–25, December 31, and January 1. Hours are subject to change.

Time needed: Thirty minutes

Admission: Tickets are reasonably priced. There are discounts for children.

Facilities: No food or toilets available on-site. Most of the site is wheelchair accessible.

Website: www.english-heritage.org.uk

The Queen's Gallery

On September 13, 1940, German bombs hit Buckingham Palace. King George IV and Queen Elizabeth escaped unharmed, but the royal chapel was not so lucky—it was demolished. In 1962, the ruined chapel was converted to a gallery exhibiting items from the monarch's public art collection. The gallery was completely refurbished in 2002.

When Buckingham Palace is not open, a visit to the Queen's Gallery provides the flavor of the palace through an extensive display of royal artwork and furnishings. But for a child, the

Queen's Gallery might be a test of patience. On weekends and holidays, family workshops and activities are conducted on-site.

WHERE? WHEN? £?

THE QUEEN'S GALLERY

Location: On the south side of Buckingham Palace, on Buckingham Palace Road

Tube: Victoria station (Circle, District, or Victoria Line)

Address: Ticket Sales and Information Office, The Official Residences of The Queen, London SW1A 1AA

Phone/email: 020 7766 7301/ bookinginfo@royalcollection.org.uk

Hours: Open every day from 10:00 a.m. to 5:30 p.m. During the summer opening of Buckingham Palace, the Queen's Gallery opens at 9:30 a.m. Last admission is one hour before closing. Closed December 25–26. Hours are subject to change.

Time needed: One hour

Admission: Tickets are reasonably priced, and there are discounts for families, students, and seniors. Children under age five get in free. Tickets can be ordered online. Limited ticket availability at the door. Combination tickets for entrance to the Royal Mews are available.

Facilities: No food available on-site. Toilets and baby-changing rooms. The site is wheelchair accessible. Back-packs and large packages must be checked at entrance.

Website: www.royal.gov.uk; www.royalcollection.org.uk

Old Dead Guys

Touring cathedrals and churches may not rank high on children's sightseeing priority lists, but if there is one ancient church in London for a family to see, it is Westminster Abbey. Or maybe St. Paul's Cathedral. Westminster Abbey is a fascinating site, drenched in history—and the same can be said for St. Paul's Cathedral. One or both deserve a spot on your itinerary.

Westminster Abbey

Kings and queens from history books are more real when you come face-to-face with their final resting places. Westminster Abbey is the final home of Henry III, Henry V, Queen Elizabeth I, and Mary Queen of Scots, as well as 3,300 other people! The roll call includes David Livingston, Isaac Newton, Charles Darwin, George Frederic Handel, and Laurence Olivier. At least one person, poet Ben Jonson, was buried standing upright; the infamous Oliver Cromwell was only a temporary resident. Cromwell's body was removed by royal decree in the mid-1600s. The oldest of the interred is Thomas Parr, whose claim to fame was that he reportedly lived for more than 152 years before being buried in the abbey in 1635.

Will so many "old dead guys" pique a child's interest? Not all of Westminster Abbey's history is ancient. Queen Elizabeth II was crowned here in 1953, and the abbey was the site of Princess Diana's funeral in 1997, the Queen Mother's funeral in 2002, and the wedding of Prince William and Kate Middleton in 2011. The abbey was also the location for a bit of action in *The Da Vinci Code*. The popular novel includes scenes featuring Sir Isaac Newton's tomb and the Chapter House in Westminster Abbey, but *The Da Vinci Code* movie was not filmed here. Westminster Abbey officials took a dim theological view of the story and refused entry to the filmmakers. The abbey also demurred in the filming of *The King's Speech*.

Although not its most glorious moment in modern history, the abbey got a nod in an episode of *The Simpsons* when Homer and Bart undertook the challenge of building a model of the elaborate landmark. Quipped Homer: "All we have to do is follow the directions."

Recent history aside, Westminster Abbey is *old*. One of the first things William the Conqueror did after taking over England was to have himself crowned in the Norman abbey that stood on the site of Westminster Abbey. That was in 1066, more than 900 years ago. Westminster Abbey was *re*built in 1245!

But again, is so much ancient history going to turn young visitors into enthusiastic tourists? One option is to pick up a copy of *A Children's Trail*—a free guidebook for kids available at the abbey's information desk. There are other ways to help prevent kids' eyes from glazing over while touring the abbey. Tell them to look up as they enter Henry VII's Lady Chapel, and they will find the banners and crests of the knights of the Order of the Bath (the clean knights). If it isn't too crowded, this is a good opportunity to take a moment, sit down, and study the variety of knights' shields and colorful banners, which incorporate a menagerie of animals, weaponry, and peculiar symbols. Kids can pick out favorites and speculate about some of the more unusual shields. Ask children what their shield would look like if they became a knight of the Order of the Bath.

There are some newer additions to Westminster Abbey. Two stained glass windows were installed in the Lady Chapel in 2013. The glass commemorates the sixtieth anniversary of Queen Elizabeth II's coronation. Another modern historical tidbit that kids can search for in Westminster Abbey is a tiny hole in the wall at the back of the Lady Chapel. The hole was blasted out during the bombing of London in World War II. It is near a memorial dedicated to Royal Air Force members who fought in the Battle of Britain. The tiny hole was the only appreciable war damage to the abbey, despite being situated just a block from the tempting targets of Parliament and other government buildings. The Royal

Air Force chapel window includes the crests from sixty-eight fighter squadrons that fought in the Battle of Britain in 1940.

Attention may turn to more old dead guys at Poet's Corner in the south transept of the abbey. Depending on their ages, kids may recognize some of the poets, writers, and actors buried and memorialized in Poet's Corner. This impressive Dead Poets' Society includes Geoffrey Chaucer, Charles Dickens, Alfred Lord Tennyson, Robert Browning, and Rudyard Kipling.

Next stop is the cloisters, a covered square of corridors once used by the abbey's monks and now filled with memorial plaques. The nearby Chapter House was the site of Parliament meetings in the fourteenth century. The College Garden is worth a look, although its hours differ from the abbey's. During summer months, lunchtime concerts are sometimes held in the garden.

Not every monument or hidden mystery in Westminster Abbey is ancient or even mysterious. Observant visitors to the abbey grounds can find one monument that official abbey guidebooks generally ignore. Thomas Crapper—the unfortunately

Westminster Abbey from Dean's Yard

named plumber—was employed here in the late 1800s to install plumbing fixtures. Several manhole covers bearing the inscription T. CRAPPER & CO. remain today around Westminster Abbey.

Westminster Abbey is so overrun with tourists that it became difficult to hold religious services because of the noise of milling crowds. So the abbey's dean instituted a program in 1997 to restore calm in the sanctuary, including controls on the size of tour groups and limits on the public tour route in Westminster Abbey. Instead of entering through the massive west doors, tourists now come in through the north doors, just off Parliament Square. The tour route includes much of the abbey, but it tries to reduce the flow of visitors walking around and through church services held in the central nave. Remember, you are visiting not a simple historic site but an active church where people come to worship and pray.

The abbey's museum is also worth a visit, if time and attention spans allow. Kids can dress up as monks in the museum.

One final note. Despite its size, Westminster Abbey is not a cathedral; it is a "royal peculiar" (there's a joke here, but we will forgo it). The term means that the abbey reports to the British monarch instead of to the normal church hierarchy of bishops and archbishops. Technically, the abbey is named the Collegiate Church of St. Peter, Westminster, but don't try asking directions using that official moniker. Of course, it's no longer really an abbey because there are no monks in residence, but there once were, and the name remains.

WHERE? WHEN? £?

WESTMINSTER ABBEY

Location: Just across the street from the Parliament building. Enter through the north doors, next to Parliament Square.

Tube: Westminster station or St. James's Park station (both on Circle or District Line)

Address: Parliament Square, London SW1

Phone/email: 020 7222 5152/info@westminster-abbey.org

Hours: Abbey: Monday, Tuesday, Thursday, and Friday from 9:30 a.m. to 3:30 p.m. On Wednesday the abbey is open until 6:00 p.m., and on Saturday the abbey is open from 9:30 a.m. to 1:30 p.m. Last admission is one hour before closing.

Chapter House: Monday through Saturday 10:30 a.m. to 4:00 p.m., closes at 3:00 p.m. on Sundays.

Pyx Chamber: Monday through Saturday 10:00 a.m. to 3:30 p.m. Closed Sundays.

Cloisters: 8:00 a.m. to 6:00 p.m. daily.

Abbey Museum: Monday through Saturday 10:30 a.m. to 4:00 p.m. Closed Sundays.

College Garden: Tuesday, Wednesday, and Thursday 10:00 a.m. to 6:00 p.m. During October through March the garden closes at 4:30 p.m.

Time needed: One to three hours

Admission: Tickets are moderately priced, and there are discounts for families, students, and seniors. Children under age eleven get in free. Admission to the Cloisters and College Garden is free. No charge for attending services.

Facilities: Cellarium Café on the abbey's grounds. Coffee and snack kiosk outside west entrance. Toilets at exit near Poet's Corner. Some areas are not wheelchair accessible.

Website: Abbey: www.westminster-abbey.org; Chapter House and Pyx Chamber: www.english-heritage.org.uk

St. Paul's Cathedral

But at last they came to St. Paul's Cathedral, which was
built a long time ago by a man with a bird's name. Wren
it was. . . . That is why so many birds live near Sir
Christopher Wren's Cathedral, which also belongs to St.
Paul, and that is why the Bird Woman lives there, too.
—*Mary Poppins*, by P. L. Travers

The original St. Paul's burned down during the Great Fire of
London in 1666, so the current cathedral is a relative newcomer
compared with Westminster Abbey. Visiting children may note
one effect of this newness: the old dead guys buried in St. Paul's
are not as old, numerous, or famous as those buried in Westminster
(they are just as dead, however). At this point in the narrative, we
offer a blanket apology to the deceased and to any readers who
are offended. In our defense, please remember that this is a book
about kids as tourists, and "old dead guys" is a realistic child's-
eye view of touring cathedrals and churches.

St. Paul's is a fitting monument to Sir Christopher Wren,
London's greatest architect. Wren is buried here (yikes, another
old dead guy!) with the simple inscription *Si monumentum requiris
circumspice*. In case your Latin is rusty, we'll translate: "If you
seek a monument, look around you." Other notables buried in
St. Paul's are the Duke of Wellington and Admiral Lord Nelson.
Gross-out note for kids: Nelson died at the Battle of Trafalgar in
1805, and his body was placed in a keg of brandy for the long trip
home. Good plan, but the sailors allegedly drank all the brandy
before they returned to home port!

One fascinating feature of the cathedral is the Whispering
Gallery. It is a long climb to reach the gallery high inside the
dome above the cathedral floor. After you catch your breath,
turn and whisper against the circular wall. Your words can
be heard on the other side of the dome, almost 130 feet away.
While in the gallery, take a look at the cathedral's frescoes.
Climb even higher to reach the Golden Gallery. This is a fantastic
observation point from which to see the entire city of London,

but the climb is long and dizzying, with almost 200 steps to the Whispering Gallery and a narrow 500 steps to the very top. American visitors may be particularly interested in the American Memorial Chapel, located behind the high altar. This is a British tribute to 28,000 Americans based in Britain who lost their lives during World War II. A book containing the names of the war dead is displayed in the chapel.

Christopher Wren wanted to rebuild the entire city of London after the Great Fire of 1666. He had even grander plans for St. Paul's Cathedral. It was not enough that the 360-foot-high dome dominated the London skyline; Wren wanted the dome to be gilded. Budget concerns nixed the gold plating, but St. Paul's dome is the second-largest church dome in the world.

One feature remains from the pre-1666 cathedral. During the fire, a statue of poet John Donne supposedly crashed through the floor and landed in the crypt below. The statue was rescued and placed in the new cathedral. Visitors today can see scorch marks on the base of the statue. St. Paul's has been tested by fire throughout the ages; an enduring image of the present cathedral is a famous photograph of St. Paul's standing intact while the surrounding section of London burns during a World War II bombing raid. Children can read about the heroic men of the cathedral's fire watch who, instead of hiding in bomb shelters during the Blitz, risked their lives putting out fires in St. Paul's. Without them, the cathedral might not have survived.

Wars, fires, and hundreds of years of wear and tear have taken their toll on Christopher Wren's masterpiece. To mark the 300th anniversary of the cathedral in 2010, St. Paul's underwent a £40 million cleaning and repair project, leaving the building in its best shape since the seventeenth century.

Admission to St. Paul's includes a multimedia guide—an upgrade to the usual audio guide found at many historic locations. A family version of the guide lets kids search for hidden secrets, answer quizzes, and play with videos and other interactive content. A cathedral full of tourists staring at video screens may

View of St. Paul's from the south side of the Thames

or may not be a good thing. For parents trying to keep children engaged, the multimedia guides may be a lifesaver. There is also a crypt (basement-level) minicinema that shows films about St. Paul's on multiple screens.

St. Paul's, like Westminster Abbey, is both a historic site and a functioning church. Although some visitors may remember the funeral of Princess Diana held in Westminster Abbey, St. Paul's was the location of Diana's wedding to Charles—a happier moment (or so it seemed at the time). Coronations are the purview of Westminster Abbey, but once enthroned, monarchs often celebrate birthdays and jubilees at St. Paul's.

St. Paul's is an active church, and it is often closed to visitors at unexpected times. During one visit to the cathedral, we were ushered out because of the arrival of hundreds of Girl Guides (the British version of Girl Scouts) attending a service to mark scouting's anniversary. Although we didn't get to see much of St. Paul's that day, it was a great opportunity for our daughter, who was a Girl Scout at the time, to make a personal connection with her English comrades.

WHERE? WHEN? £?

ST. PAUL'S CATHEDRAL

Location: On Ludgate Hill, just north of the Thames, about halfway between Parliament and the Tower of London

Tube: St. Paul's station (Central Line)

Address: St. Paul's Cathedral, St. Paul's Churchyard, London EC4M 8AD

Phone/email: 020 7246 8357/ admissions@stpaulscathedral.org.uk

Hours: Cathedral is open to visitors Monday through Saturday from 8:30 a.m. to 4:30 p.m. Last admission thirty minutes before closing. Galleries are open from 9:30 a.m. to 4:15 p.m.

Time needed: One or two hours

Admission: Tickets are moderately priced, and there are discounts for children, families, students, and seniors. Children under age six get in free. Tickets can be purchased at the cathedral, but there is a discount for online booking, and online tickets provide fast-track entry.

Facilities: Café and restaurant (no outside food allowed). Toilets and baby-changing areas. Most areas are wheelchair accessible.

Website: www.stpauls.co.uk

Big Wigs

Y ou won't find many wigs in Parliament these days—the Whig party of British politics is long gone, morphed and merged into the current Liberal Party. Wigs were the uniform here, but changing fashions and parliamentary reform have done away with the image of sonorous, bewigged parliamentarians. Children who have studied government in school may be interested in visiting Britain's Houses of Parliament. If not, parents who want to see Parliament can always remind kids that it is a chance to explore the building where Big Ben is located.

Parliament and Big Ben

Not to shatter any illusions, but Big Ben is not really Big Ben. This symbol of London is actually the clock tower of the Palace of Westminster; "Big Ben" simply refers to the bell inside the tower. That architectural fact hardly stops people from calling the tower Big Ben, though. The origin of the nickname is not clear, but some historians claim that the clock was named after Sir Benjamin Hall, a supervisor during the construction of the tower. In 2012, to mark the Diamond Jubilee of Queen Elizabeth II, the tower was officially renamed the Elizabeth Tower. Sorry, Your Majesty, everyone still calls it "Big Ben."

Although the Parliament building interior is interesting, the historical trivia associated with the building is fascinating. In the House of Commons chamber, visitors learn the origin of the expression "to toe the line": a line is marked on the floor of the chamber; no matter how vehement the debate, opposing speakers may not step across this line. The line is located so that more than a sword's length separates opposing members. Today, disorderly conduct can still be a problem in the chamber, and the House of Commons' sergeant-at-arms has extraordinary powers to maintain the peace, including the authority to issue an arrest warrant for anyone in the country and imprison the unfortunate individual for up to five years without possibility of appeal. You do not want to cross this guy, so toe the line!

Between the House of Commons and House of Lords, the central dome's gold murals depict four saints representing the four sections of the United Kingdom: Saint David for Wales, Saint Patrick for Ireland, Saint Andrew for Scotland, and Saint George for England. Another impressive architectural feature of Parliament is the huge, medieval Westminster Hall. This is the oldest surviving piece of the original Westminster Palace, built in 1097. Unlike some restored ancient buildings, Westminster Hall actually looks like a medieval hall, with a high hammer beam ceiling and dark, smoke-stained atmosphere. There are no elaborate furnishings, no bright gold ornamentation, just the cold stonework and a dark wood ceiling.

Because of security concerns and the need to keep tourists from bothering members while the legislature is in session, full access to Parliament is limited. British citizens can often get building passes through their MPs (members of Parliament). When Parliament is in session, foreign visitors are not allowed to tour the buildings, and they are limited to what were once called "strangers galleries" in both houses of Parliament. Beginning in 2004, the visiting public was no longer referred to as strangers, and the galleries are now known as the "public galleries." How democratic!

Understanding how best to tour Parliament is no simple task. Not long after Buckingham Palace opened to summer visitors, Parliament began its own summer openings. The openings are usually held in August and September, and they are the easiest way for an overseas visitor to tour Parliament. Tours are also offered on Saturdays throughout the year. There are occasional Friday evening guided tours of the House of Lords and daytime tours of the portrait gallery in the House of Commons' modern Portcullis House.

Generally, Parliament is in session Monday through Thursday with lots of holiday breaks—politicians being the same everywhere, they need plenty of time to schmooze with the electorate back home. The liveliest time to visit is during Question Time, when members verbally parry and the opposition tries to zing the prime minister. Question Time is so popular that only British citizens with tickets stand a chance of getting in, although overseas visitors are admitted if space is available.

Tourists without advance tickets can line up outside St. Stephen's entrance to Parliament, but a wait of one or two hours is common. Sometimes it is easier to get in during the late afternoon or early evening, or on a Friday. When Parliament is in session, there are separate lines for entering the House of Commons and the House of Lords. How can you tell if Parliament is in session? If the tower opposite Big Ben has a flag flying, Parliament is in session. If you can't get into Parliament, you can at least visit an exhibit on the history of Parliament in the nearby fourteenth-century Jewel Tower, part of the old Palace of Westminster.

When all is said and done, the question remains: will kids enjoy a tour of Parliament? The answer is a definite maybe. There are no interactive exhibits here (thumbs down), but no old dead guys, either (thumbs up).

Parliament and its famous clock tower

Where? When? £?

Parliament/Palace of Westminster

Location: Next to the Thames, in Westminster. Find Big Ben and you've found Parliament.

Tube: Westminster station (Circle or District Line)

Address: House of Commons, London SW1A 0AA; House of Lords, London SW1A 0PW

Phone/email: Commons Information: 020 7219 4272/hcinfo@parliament.uk; Lords Information: 020 7219 3107/hlinfo@parliament.uk

Hours: Guided tours on most Saturdays year-round from 9:15 a.m. to 4:30 p.m. Summer openings vary, but generally are from the end of July through August. Tours start at 1:15 p.m. on Monday and at 9:30 a.m. Tuesday through Saturday. Tours end at 4:30 p.m. There is often a late-September opening with slightly different hours.

Generally the House of Commons Public Gallery is open Monday from 2:30 p.m. to 10:30 p.m., Tuesday and Wednesday from 11:30 a.m. to 7:30 p.m., Thursday from 9:30 a.m. to 6:30 p.m., and Friday (when in session) from 9:30 a.m. to 3:00 p.m. Hours for the House of Lords vary but are similar. Can these hours change? Of course—they are set by politicians. It is best to check the Parliament website.

Time needed: Depends on how long you have to wait in line. Tours last seventy-five minutes.

Admission: When Parliament is in session, admission is free. Summer opening tickets are moderately priced, and there are discounts for children and seniors. Children under age four get in free. Tickets are available at the ticket office located on Abingdon Green, across Abingdon Street from Parliament, or online.

Facilities: Toilets and baby-changing areas. No coat or bag check. Most areas are wheelchair accessible.

Website: www.parliament.uk

WHERE? WHEN? £?

PARLIAMENT PAST AND PRESENT EXHIBIT

Location: Jewel Tower, just across the street from Parliament buildings

Tube: Westminster station (Circle or District Line)

Address: Abingdon Street, Westminster, London SW1P 3JX

Phone: 020 7222 2219

Hours: From the end of March through early November, the Jewel Tower is open daily from 10:00 a.m. to 5:00 p.m. In other months, the site is generally open Saturday and Sunday from 10:00 a.m. to 4:00 p.m. Last admission is thirty minutes before closing. Closed December 24–26, December 31–January 1. Hours subject to change.

Time needed: Fifteen to thirty minutes

Admission: Tickets are inexpensive, and there are discounts for children.

Facilities: Coffee shop on-site. Parts of the site are not wheelchair accessible.

Website: www.english-heritage.org.uk

Parliamentary Side Trips — In Search of Abe Lincoln and Ben Franklin

It is a long way from a Kentucky log cabin to the London borough of Westminster, but President Abraham Lincoln made the trip (at least in effigy). A statue of "Honest Abe" stands in Parliament Square near Westminster Abbey. This is hardly a major tourist attraction, but it makes an interesting footnote, and seeing Lincoln's statue is one way that American children can make a London connection to US history. In fact, statues of famous Americans are fairly common in London. George Washington's statue is located in front of the National Gallery; Franklin Roosevelt and Winston Churchill share a park bench at the end of Grafton Street; another statue of FDR stands in Grosvenor Square near a statue of Dwight Eisenhower. Roosevelt and Eisenhower were joined in 2011 by a larger-than-life statue of Ronald Reagan.

One famous American hero spent more time in London than Lincoln, Washington, Roosevelt, and Eisenhower combined. Benjamin Franklin lived for almost eighteen years at a house on Craven Street, about a half-mile north of Parliament. While in London, Franklin (a "big Ben" in his own time) invented a twenty-four-hour clock and bifocal glasses. His efforts at diplomacy proved less successful, and Franklin beat a hasty retreat from London in 1775 just ahead of war between Britain and the American colonies.

After Franklin's departure, the house served as an anatomy school (specimens are on display), hotel, and office space. The building fell into disrepair, but the Benjamin Franklin House was restored in 2006 and opened to the public for interpretative tours and as an educational center.

Costumed guide at the Benjamin Franklin House

If Benjamin Franklin were reincarnated today he would instantly recognize 36 Craven Street, especially the building's interior, restored to its mid-1700s appearance. The Benjamin Franklin House emphasizes experiences rather than artifacts to transport visitors into Franklin's world. A costumed guide escorts guests through the house while interacting with sound and video snippets portraying Franklin's life in London. The hands-on educational center offers visitors the chance to learn about Franklin's contributions to science. The center is open to groups by appointment.

WHERE? WHEN? £?

BENJAMIN FRANKLIN HOUSE

Location: On Craven Street, just east of Trafalgar Square

Tube: Charing Cross station (Bakerloo or Northern Line)

Address: 36 Craven Street, London WC2N 5NF

Phone: 020 7839 2006

Hours: Historical experience shows are held hourly Wednesday through Sunday from 12:00 noon to 4:15 p.m. Guided building tours are given on Monday. Box office is open from 10:30 a.m. to 5:00 p.m. every day except Tuesday.

Time needed: One hour

Admission: Tickets are reasonably priced, and there are discounts for children and students. Tickets can be booked online.

Facilities: None. Not wheelchair accessible.

Website: www.benjaminfranklinhouse.org

Flowers and Buskers

The Covent Garden Market figures prominently in the 1964 musical *My Fair Lady,* whose central character, Eliza Doolittle, is a nineteenth-century flower girl. But Covent Garden's history, like most of London's, is much older. In medieval times, monks from Westminster Abbey grew and sold vegetables in this area, and the name Covent Garden is supposedly a corruption of convent garden—a reference to the abbey.

There were fruit, vegetable, and flower markets at Covent Garden from the medieval era until 1974. When the markets moved out, they were replaced by the modern incarnation of Covent Garden: an entertaining variety of shops, cafés, and restaurants. The area houses an eclectic collection of stores, pubs, theaters, and a museum or two. In a return to its origins, Covent Garden sometimes holds an elaborate flower festival in June, featuring landscapes, flower displays, and demonstration gardens along with themed art events and performances at nearby churches and other venues.

Covent Garden Market

On any summer afternoon or evening, visitors will find a variety of street performers, or *buskers,* in the piazza near the old market. The shows are free, but drop some pence into the hat if you appreciate the entertainment. Over several trips, our kids gawked at fire-eaters, a man who danced and spun on his head (wearing a helmet), and a thick-skinned individual who lay down on a bed of nails and invited an audience member to walk on his stomach. Does the admonition "Don't try this at home" sound familiar?

Covent Garden's reputation for street performances goes back a long time. In 1642, famed British diarist Samuel Pepys wrote about seeing a Punch and Judy marionette show at Covent Garden.

Inside the Covent Garden central market building, which looks vaguely like an old train station, you'll find more costly retail entertainment. The merchants operating in Covent Garden have become a bit less unique in recent years as corporate giants like Apple, Disney, and Gap have muscled aside some independent retailers. Despite this trend, Covent Garden retains enough of its quirkiness to distinguish itself from the average mall or marketplace.

Weather permitting, some of Covent Garden's cafés serve meals al fresco. The food varies in type, quality, and cost, but this is generally a good place to find kid-friendly fare. Covent Garden has a number of full-fledged restaurants, such as Orso, an upscale Italian eatery with another location in New York City.

Covent Garden is more than just an old marketplace, however. The streets around this area, especially northwest toward Seven Dials, are a warren of shops, bars, and restaurants. Stop by Neil's Yard Dairy for high-cholesterol treat; it offers one of the most extensive cheese selections in the city.

Old and new technologies converge at Covent Garden

For a break from the hustle and bustle of the area, buy some takeaway food from the marketplace and seek out a quiet bench in the churchyard of St. Paul's Church. This unassuming little building is known as the Actors' Church because of its long-standing association with the theater community in Covent Garden and the nearby West End theater district.

After dark, especially on weekends, the crowds around Covent Garden are full of young bar-hoppers. Some spill out onto the streets; the crowds can be a little disconcerting when walking through the area with young children, but the revelers are generally unthreatening. On some summer weekends, the area is so overrun with tourists and partiers that Transport for London restricts access to the Covent Garden Tube station. Not to worry—it is an easy walk to Leicester Square, or even to Trafalgar Square, where you can catch the Tube or a bus.

Transport Museum

Right next to Covent Garden's central market is a museum that attracts children like a magnet. Where else in London can kids get behind the controls of a subway train and take a virtual journey

Hands-on at the London Transport Museum

through the tunnels of London's Tube? At the Transport Museum, kids and adults can climb on old trams and buses, "drive" several vintages of Tube trains, and buy popular London Transport souvenirs. The museum employs costumed actors who interact with (and occasionally startle) young visitors.

The Transport Museum has areas where younger children can push buttons, spin signs, and generally touch and play with everything. A complete renovation in 2007 took what was already one of the most popular attractions in Covent Garden and transformed it into an even more family-friendly venue. There are new galleries, simulators, and extra room to display more of the buses, trams, and other conveyances from the Transport Museum's huge collection.

All Aboard! is designed to let children under age six climb onto scaled-down versions of a bus, Tube train, and taxi. The Interchange is a hands-on exploration area for seven- to eleven-year-olds. The museum also features a drop-in activity room where kids can grab some crayons and color transportation-related pictures. The museum's shop is the place to purchase popular Transport for London merchandise. If your kids love buses, streetcars, and subways, the Transport Museum is worth a visit.

WHERE? WHEN? £?

TRANSPORT MUSEUM

Location: The east (Russell Street) end of the piazza that surrounds Covent Garden Market
Tube: Covent Garden station (Piccadilly Line)
Address: Covent Garden Piazza, London WC2E 7BB
Phone/email: General information: 020 7379 6344; Recorded information: 020 7565 7299/enquiry@ ltmuseum.co.uk
Hours: The museum is open every day except Friday from 10:00 a.m. to 6:00 p.m. Friday hours are

11:00 a.m. to 6:00 p.m. Last admission is 5:15 p.m.
Closed December 24–26. Expect lines during summer
months and school holidays.
Time needed: At least an hour
Admission: Tickets are moderately priced, and
children under age sixteen get in free. There are discounts for students and seniors. Tickets are valid for
unlimited visits for twelve months.
Facilities: Café on-site. Toilets and baby-changing
areas. Most areas are wheelchair accessible.
Website: www.ltmuseum.co.uk

Royal Opera House

The Royal Opera House is located just behind Covent Garden
Market. Most performances here are intended for adults, but
occasionally the Royal Opera offers programs for children. Check
the opera's website at www.roh.org.uk.

War and Peace

The grand old Duke of York,
He had ten thousand men;
He marched them up to the top of the hill
And he marched them down again!
—Traditional children's song

Churchill War Rooms

Bombs away! If your kids are interested in World War II (and even if they're not), the Churchill War Rooms may prove fascinating to them. The war rooms were the underground headquarters of Winston Churchill during the Blitz attacks on London.

Most kids enjoy exploring hidden areas, so the whole family will likely enjoy meandering through the warren of underground conference rooms, passageways, sleeping quarters, communications centers, and map rooms. For a little education along with your exploration, use the audio headphones provided free with each admission. There is a special audio tour for kids, and the War Rooms' website has a downloadable trail map for children. The commentary isn't boring, and listening to it slows down kids who tend to fast-forward through historical displays.

The Churchill War Rooms are more interesting than the average museum, and children may actually learn something about World War II after spending some time here. Kids might already know a bit about the war from school, movies, or older relatives, but their details are often vague.

The Churchill War Rooms are historically authentic. After the war ended, many of the rooms were closed off and left untouched for years. The Imperial War Museum, which operates the Churchill War Rooms, has done a thorough job of restoring the site to its wartime appearance.

Almost the entire wartime underground complex is open to the public. The Churchill family's private quarters include Mrs. Churchill's bedroom, a private dining room, and a kitchen. The museum transports visitors through Churchill's life, although it's not a strictly chronological review. Instead, the museum presents five thematic chapters: Young Churchill, War Leader, Cold War Statesman, Maverick Politician, and Wilderness Years.

There's more British historical detail here than the average non-British visitor may wish to absorb, and the Churchill Museum may be a bit dry for some children. But the museum makes use of computer and video technology to enliven that history for the

The Lifeline charts Churchill's life and career

casual visitor while allowing history buffs to delve deeper into the story. The spine of the museum is Lifeline, a fifty-foot-long video table that presents an interactive timeline of Churchill's life. Visitors can explore more than 300 data points, encountering some programmed "Easter egg" surprises that will delight, or at least startle, those gathered around the huge video screen.

The museum even interactively captures a few of Churchill's personality quirks. The man was fond of the carp stocked in the fishpond at his family home, and would dangle his hand on the water's surface, where the fish would gently nibble his fingers. The museum has a tiny "pond," and electronic fish appear when a visitor touches the Plexiglas surface.

Churchill ranks as one of the most quotable speakers of the twentieth century, and the museum resounds with recordings of his speeches. Exhibits include an Enigma machine that helped break German wartime codes (as seen in the 2014 movie *The Imitation Game*). Churchill referred to this machine as "the geese that laid the golden eggs." Other artifacts include Churchill's odd-looking siren suit: custom-made velvet engineer's coveralls that he preferred as casual wear. Uniforms, document reproductions, and a model of Churchill's Chartwell home are also on display. Near the end of the museum stands the front door to No. 10 Downing Street, a poignant reminder of the man who twice served as prime minister.

This museum was called the Cabinet War Rooms until 2005. That year, when the Churchill Museum was opened, the venue was relabeled Cabinet War Rooms and Churchill Museum. In 2010, the moniker was shortened to the Churchill War Rooms.

WHERE? WHEN? £?

CHURCHILL WAR ROOMS

Location: Underneath the Treasury Building, just off Horse Guards Parade Road across from St. James's Park
Tube: Westminster station (Circle, District, or Jubilee Line)
Address: Clive Steps, King Charles Street, London SW1A 2AQ
Phone/email: 020 7930 6961/cwr@iwm.org.uk
Hours: Open daily from 9:30 a.m. to 6:00 p.m. Last admission at 5:00 p.m. Closed December 24–26.
Time needed: One to two hours
Admission: Tickets are moderately priced, and children age fifteen and under get in free. There are discounts for students and seniors. Tickets can be booked online through the museum's website or purchased on-site.
Facilities: Café (no outside food allowed). Toilets and baby-changing areas. The museum is wheelchair accessible.
Website: www.iwm.org.uk

Imperial War Museum London

London has an entire museum devoted to war—the Imperial War Museum. The museum tries not to glamorize war—in fact, there are a few fairly graphic exhibits, such as the Holocaust Exhibition, that are not suitable for younger children. What the Imperial War Museum does offer is a wealth of interesting hardware: guns, tanks, airplanes, and rockets.

To commemorate the centenary of World War I (1914–1918), the Imperial War Museum underwent a major transformation with the opening of First World War Galleries. A Life at the Front exhibit provides a realistic depiction of the sights and sounds of life and death in World War I trenches. This area displays an iconic Sopwith Camel biplane and a once-lumbering Mark V tank. The museum's soaring atrium has been reconfigured for dramatic large displays, including a Harrier jet, a Spitfire fighter plane, a Russian tank, and a V-2 rocket.

World War II had a devastating impact on many London residents. What was it like to live through war in London? The exhibit A Family in Wartime traces the experiences of an ordinary family who endured wartime rationing, evacuation of their children,

The Imperial War Museum's large exhibit hall

and bombings of their south London home. The exhibit makes history personal—lessons that won't be lost on modern families.

The Imperial War Museum gives visitors a British perspective of World War II. Britain's defeat at Dunkirk, the Blitz, and the Battle of Britain become much more real after a visit to the Imperial War Museum.

WHERE? WHEN? £?

IMPERIAL WAR MUSEUM LONDON

Location: On the south bank of the Thames, southeast of Parliament

Tube: Lambeth North station (Bakerloo Line) or Elephant and Castle station (Northern Line)

Address: Lambeth Road, London SE1 6HZ

Phone/email: 020 7416 5000/mail@iwm.org.uk

Hours: Open from 10:00 a.m. to 6:00 p.m. daily. Last admission is 5:45 p.m. Closed December 24–26.

Time needed: Two hours

Admission: Free

Facilities: Café with children's menus, outside picnic area. Toilets and baby-changing areas. Most areas of the museum are wheelchair accessible.

Website: www.iwm.org.uk

Florence Nightingale Museum

Lo! in that house of misery,
A lady with a lamp I see,
Pass through the glimmering gloom,
And flit from room to room.
—"Santa Filomena," by Henry Wadsworth Longfellow

The Florence Nightingale Museum portrays another side of warfare—that of mercy and dedication in the face of misery. Florence Nightingale was the "lady with a lamp," a heroic British nurse during and after the Crimean War.

The museum's collection displays artifacts from that conflict, Nightingale's childhood, and her later life as a health reform campaigner. The museum includes modern interactive displays. Kids can don stethoscopes and listen at audio hot spots scattered throughout the exhibits.

This little museum is popular with school groups and can occasionally be crowded. At other times, this is a low-key and worthwhile stop for children or adults who are interested in nursing and in the Florence Nightingale story.

WHERE? WHEN? £?

FLORENCE NIGHTINGALE MUSEUM

Location: South Bank, right across the river from Parliament, on the site of St. Thomas' Hospital

Tube: Waterloo station (Bakerloo, Jubilee, Northern, or Waterloo & City Line), or use Westminster station (Circle or District Line) and walk over Westminster Bridge

Address: 2 Lambeth Palace Road, London SE1 7EW

Phone/email: 020 7620 0374/ info@florence-nightingale.co.uk

Hours: Open daily from 10:00 a.m. to 5:00 p.m. Last admission is one hour before closing. Closed Good Friday and December 24–25.

Time needed: One hour

Admission: Tickets are reasonably priced. There are discounts for families, children, students, and seniors.

Facilities: Toilets on-site. The museum is wheelchair accessible.

Website: www.florence-nightingale.co.uk

Florence Nightingale on duty

Museums — Some Serious, Some Not

He gazed and gazed and gazed and gazed,
Amazed, amazed, amazed, amazed.
—"Rhyme for a Child Viewing a Naked Venus
in a Painting," by Robert Browning

When we planned our first London trip, our family decided to avoid spending valuable vacation time on things we could do at home. That ruled out eating at McDonald's, Pizza Hut, and the Hard Rock Café. There are lots of department stores at home too, so we gave them only a passing visit in London. In addition, because our kids had toured a fair number of museums at home, we decided to visit only a few museums in London.

Realistically, most kids have little patience to devote to art exhibits and museums. When you plan to visit museums in London, consider limiting the time you spend in the museums and the number of things you try to see in each. Be prepared to miss a lot; kids often fast-forward through museums, leaving placard-reading parents in their wake. Satisfy yourself with seeing the highlights and getting the flavor of each museum. With luck, you will return to London and see more when the kids are older or tour London's museums without the children in the future.

London has dozens of museums, some more interesting to families than others. We'll get you started with this handful:

- The world-renowned British Museum, located in north-central London
- A cluster of three very different museums—Natural History, Science, and Victoria and Albert—in South Kensington
- The Museum of London, near London's financial district
- The Museum in Docklands

- The Victoria and Albert Museum of Childhood—a museum devoted to toys
- A museum dedicated to the world-famous fictional detective Sherlock Holmes
- The Tate Modern and the National Gallery, for families who want to venture into art museums

British Museum

When I first came up to London I had rooms in Montague Street, just around the corner from the British Museum, and there I waited, filling in my too abundant leisure time by studying all those branches of science which might make me more efficient.

—*The Memoirs of Sherlock Holmes*, by Sir Arthur Conan Doyle

The British Museum is the most famous museum in England—perhaps in the world—and it has a lot to offer from a kid's perspective. But the British Museum is so huge that it can overwhelm visiting families and quickly go from a thrilling experience to a tiring one. Here are some survival strategies. Focus on a few museum highlights, pick a theme, or look for things that appeal to your child's special interests. Or you can sign up for a ninety-minute guided highlights tour. The British Museum's website has an extensive and interactive Young Explorers section.

Read up on the British Museum before you go. Nothing is quite as pathetic as tourists with young children standing in the lobby, studying a map, trying to decide which way to head in this vast museum. The kids start getting antsy, the parents become frazzled, and the visit is off to a bad start. One high-tech solution is to rent children's multimedia guides or take advantage of low-tech options and pick up free family trail guides or activity backpacks from the Families desk in the Great Court.

The British Museum was founded in 1753, making even the museum a "museum piece." Despite its age, the British Museum continues to evolve. It has long-standing permanent displays from Egypt, western Asia, Greece, and Rome; prehistoric and Roman-era British items; and extensive medieval, Renaissance, modern, and Oriental collections. At one time, the British Library shared space here, but it moved to separate quarters in 1997. With the added space, the British Museum made major changes in its Great Hall exhibition area. By enclosing a center courtyard, the museum was able to add an education center.

Although most museums have strict hands-off policies concerning their exhibits, the British Museum features Hands On areas. Located in the central Reading Room and other areas of the museum, Hands On offers a chance to touch and examine a select (and presumably sturdy) sample of ancient artifacts. The museum's Digital Discovery Centre is an attempt to bridge the gap between traditional museum concepts and the digital age. The center offers weekend activities geared to families with children age five and older.

The Great Court at the British Museum

WHERE? WHEN? £?

BRITISH MUSEUM

Location: Bloomsbury, north of New Oxford Street
Tube: Tottenham Court Road station (Central or Northern Line), Russell Square station (Piccadilly Line), or Holborn station (Central or Piccadilly Line)

Address: Great Russell Street, London WC1 3DG
Phone/email: 020 7323 8299/
information@britishmuseum.org
Hours: Museum galleries are open daily from 10:00
a.m. to 5:30 p.m. Open Friday until 8:30 p.m. Some individual exhibits have shorter hours. The Great Court is
open daily from 9:00 a.m. to 6:00 p.m. and Friday until
8:30 p.m. Closed December 24-26 and January 1.
Time needed: How patient are your children? Visitors
can skim the highlights in two hours or spend days here.
Admission: Free except for some special exhibits
Facilities: Restaurant and cafés (no outside food
allowed); family picnic area is open on weekends. Baby-changing areas, nursing area. Coat checks. Most of the
museum is wheelchair accessible.
Website: www.britishmuseum.org

Natural History Museum

There are natural history museums of stature in many major cities, and London is no exception. Although there is nothing uniquely British about the concept of this museum, the London version is superb. With subjects encompassing volcanoes, dinosaurs, and ecology, natural history is a natural magnet for children. But like many museums, London's Natural History Museum must compete for the attention of children and adults who are used to seeing elaborate computer graphics and animation. The Natural History Museum succeeds in getting a "wow" out of visitors who have seen dinosaurs come to life through the magic of computer-generated imagery.

The museum's exhibits include some realistic animated dinosaurs, a simulated womb, and a Creepy Crawlies exhibit for anthropoid lovers. A huge model of a blue whale is suspended overhead in one room, and visitors can experience a simulated earthquake in a different area. Some mild cautions: the dinosaurs are munching on a less fortunate fellow; the human biology exhibit may evoke some interesting questions from younger children; if spiders make you uncomfortable, Creepy Crawlies is not for you. The whale is tame, though, and the earthquake is fun.

The museum's Darwin Centre houses 22 million specimens—sometimes referred to as "gross stuff in jars"—collected on the voyages of Captain James Cook, Charles Darwin, and countless other scientists. Kids can get a close-up look at this pickled menagerie on a behind-the-scenes tour. The Darwin Centre's display of insects is housed in a modernistic podlike building filled with interactive exhibits that practically bring the collection of dead bugs to life.

Not all the specimens at the Natural History Museum are dead, though. The wildlife garden features butterflies, animals, plants, and birds—all very much alive and on display near the museum's west entrance from April through October. Wintertime visitors can rent skates and glide around the museum's outdoor ice-skating rink, open late October through early January. The rink is one of several that operates seasonally near major London attractions.

Like the British Museum, the Natural History Museum hosts special events for children and families, including tours, workshops, and even puppet shows. Check the museum's website for the latest offerings. Children under age seven can borrow an explorer

New Darwin Centre joins old Natural History Museum

backpack, complete with pith helmet and binoculars. The museum has a hands-on science lab designed for kids ages seven to fourteen. The Investigate Lab lets children use computers, microscopes, and other scientific tools to explore animal, plant, and geological specimens. Parents can also purchase Discovery Guides in versions for kids ages five to seven and eight to eleven.

WHERE? WHEN? £?

NATURAL HISTORY MUSEUM

Location: In Kensington, just south of Hyde Park
Tube: South Kensington station (Piccadilly, Circle, or District Line)
Address: Cromwell Road, London SW7 5BD

Phone/email: 020 7942 5000/ information@nhm.ac.uk
Hours: Open daily from 10:00 a.m. to 5:50 p.m. Last admission is 5:30 p.m. Closed December 24–26.
Time needed: Several hours. Lines on summer weekends can be long, especially for the dinosaur exhibit.
Admission: Free except for some special exhibits
Facilities: Restaurant, cafés, and snack bar; indoor and outdoor picnic areas. Toilets and baby-changing areas. Coat check. Most of the museum is wheelchair accessible.
Website: www.nhm.ac.uk

Victoria and Albert Museum

The Fossil sisters lived in the Cromwell Road. At that end of it which is farthest away from the Brompton Road, and yet sufficiently near it so one could be taken to look at the dolls' houses in the Victoria and Albert every wet day. If the weather were not too wet, one was expected to "save the penny and walk."

—*Ballet Shoes*, by Noel Streatfeild

From a child's perspective, the Victoria and Albert Museum, dedicated to the decorative arts, is a stark contrast to its neighbors, the Science and Natural History Museums. Go ahead, ask your children if they want to tour a museum featuring exhibits on the history of fashion, textiles, ceramics, and jewelry. The answer may be no, especially when that museum is so close to all the cool stuff in the Science and Natural History Museums.

Yet the Victoria and Albert Museum staff deserve credit because they try to interest children. Young visitors can borrow activity backpacks at the museum's front desk. The backpacks relate to different areas of the museum and contain tactile activities (discovering objects by feel while blindfolded), a museum treasure hunt, and other fun things for kids to do. Nothing can turn the V&A into a children's museum, but the backpacks make a family visit manageable. A family trail guide outlines a treasure trail that kids can follow through the museum; an activity cart for children is available on Sundays and some school holidays; and hands-on exhibits are scattered throughout the museum. In nice weather, children can splash in the V&A's shallow courtyard reflecting pool (assuming it's okay with their parents).

WHERE? WHEN? £?

VICTORIA AND ALBERT MUSEUM

Location: In Kensington, just south of Hyde Park, near the Natural History Museum
Tube: South Kensington station (Piccadilly, Circle, or District Line)
Address: Cromwell Road, London SW7 2RL
Phone/email: 020 7942 2000/vanda@vam.ac.uk
Hours: Open daily from 10:00 a.m. to 5:45 p.m. Open Friday until 10:00 p.m. Closed December 24–26.
Time needed: An hour or less with kids in tow; longer if patience allows

Admission: Free
Facilities: Café and restaurant; indoor and outdoor picnic spots. Toilets and baby-changing areas/nursing room. Coat and package check. Most areas of the museum are wheelchair accessible.
Website: ww.vam.ac.uk

Science Museum

Visit London's Science Museum and you may have a problem: once children get inside this museum, they may refuse to leave! The focus of the Science Museum is high tech, hands-on, interactive, and up-to-date, with just a smidgen of history.

The displays grab a child's attention like no other museum in the city. Start with the Launchpad, which looks like a giant indoor playground. Kids playing here may not realize that the Launchpad is really a huge physics lab. Exhibits cover fluid dynamics, suspension construction, weight, force, and other physical properties. Kids don't just look at the exhibits or press a few buttons—they climb on machines and make them work.

There's an undercurrent of cooperative play here, because several of the experiments will function only if children join together in a group effort. A model rocket spins around overhead, but it works only if four kids synchronize four air pumps. A conveyor belt/lift contraption moves beans from one end to the other with the cooperation of five or six operators. There are dozens of stations in the Launchpad, so it can accommodate a large crowd of kids, and they can all put their hands on something.

The Launchpad is appropriate for children age eight and older (and their parents!), but the museum has not forgotten younger kids. The basement garden is an interactive area where three- to six-year-olds can experiment through play. Pattern Pod is another favorite gallery for kids ages five to eight. There's an admission charge for the flight and space simulator rides that add a bit of amusement park excitement to the Science Museum.

The museum employs unusual materials to construct familiar objects and presents familiar objects in unusual ways. In the middle of the area devoted to materials, suspended from the ceiling, is the framework of a house. A bridge made almost entirely of glass traverses the gallery; on quiet days, visitors walking across the bridge can hear it "sing" harmonically in response to their footsteps.

The Science Museum is a popular destination for school groups, and it can get a little crowded at times. If you are visiting while British schools are in session, plan to arrive early or late in the day. The museum offers indoor areas where groups can eat brown bag lunches without overrunning the museum's café. The café is an acceptable place for a snack or light lunch; it serves special box lunches for kids.

The Science Museum does not rest on its laurels. The museum is constantly updating its displays. So when you finally drag your kids out of the museum, you can promise a return visit on a future trip to see what's new.

WHERE? WHEN? £?

SCIENCE MUSEUM

Location: Just south of Hyde Park, near the Victoria and Albert Museum

Tube: South Kensington station (Piccadilly, Circle, or District Line)

Address: Exhibition Road, South Kensington, London SW7 2DD

Phone/email: 020 7942 4000/feedback@nmsi.ac.uk

Hours: 10:00 a.m. to 6:00 p.m. daily. Open until 7:00 p.m. during school holidays (usually a week near the end of May, October, February, and December, plus much of the summer). Last admission is forty-five minutes before closing. Closed December 24–26.

Time needed: Several hours

Admission: Free. Special exhibits and the IMAX Cinema cost extra. Family passes are available.

Facilities: Several restaurants, indoor picnic area.
Toilets and baby-changing areas. Unattended coat check.
Most areas of the museum are wheelchair accessible.
Website: www.sciencemuseum.org.uk

Museum of London

London is chock-full of museums dedicated to various forms of art and history. The Museum of London takes an introspective view—the subject is London itself; the museum examines the city from prehistory to the present day. This modern museum provides visitors a history lesson, showing glimpses of old London from Roman artifacts to re-created eighteenth-century prison cells. Kids peer with morbid fascination at the diorama and video depicting the Great Fire of London.

One of the museum's prize displays is the lord mayor's coach. The coach is elaborate, but if you have already visited the Royal Mews at Buckingham Palace, you may have seen enough ceremonial coaches for one trip. The Museum of London is a good rainy-day venue for older children and adults. The museum's well-designed displays use an interactive timeline to trace the history of London from pre-Roman times to the present. The Sackler Hall on the lower level has computers where visitors can learn more about the museum's massive inventory of London-related objects.

The museum's artifacts from the abandoned Roman city of Londinium are fascinating. The Museum of London is built along the old Roman city wall, a portion of which forms one side of the museum's inner courtyard.

WHERE? WHEN? £?

MUSEUM OF LONDON

Location: A couple of blocks north of St. Paul's Cathedral
Tube: Barbican station (Circle or Metropolitan Line)

Address: 150 London Wall, London EC2Y 5HN
Phone/email: 020 7001 9844/
info@museumoflondon.org.uk
Hours: Open daily from 10:00 a.m. to 6:00 p.m. Closed
December 24–26.
Time needed: One or two hours
Admission: Free
Facilities: Restaurant, indoor picnic area. Toilets and
baby-changing areas. Coat check. Museum is wheelchair
accessible.
Website: www.museumoflondon.org.uk

Museum in Docklands

A great deal of London's history revolves around its position
at the center of Britain's seagoing empire. The Museum of
London operates the Museum in Docklands, housed in a restored
200-year-old Georgian warehouse at Canary Wharf. The museum
contains countless artifacts that tell the story of the Docklands,
warehouses, and trade, including a permanent exhibition on slave
trade: London, Sugar, & Slavery.

The museum's Sailortown gallery is a full-scale re-creation
of the dark and dubious local streetscape frequented by sailors
in the mid-1800s, but the Mudlarks gallery may be more interesting to kids. Mudlarks are people who search the muddy banks
of the Thames looking for treasure, usually finding junk but
occasionally unearthing valuable artifacts. The Mudlarks gallery
contains a play area for younger kids and interactive exhibits for
older children. Despite the "dirty" name, no actual mud digging
is involved. Be sure to pick up (free) timed entry Mudlarks gallery
tickets as you enter the museum.

WHERE? WHEN? £?

MUSEUM IN DOCKLANDS

Location: Docklands, east of the Tower of London
Transportation: West India Quay (Docklands Light Railway) or Canary Warf (Jubilee Line)
Address: No. 1 Warehouse, West India Quay, Canary Wharf, London E14 4AL
Phone/email: 020 7001 9844/ info.docklands@museumoflondon.org.uk
Hours: Open daily from 10:00 a.m. to 6:00 p.m. Mudlarks gallery open 2:00 p.m. to 5:30 p.m. on weekdays; 10:30 a.m. to 5:30 p.m. on weekends and school holidays. Closed December 24–26.
Time needed: One to two hours
Admission: Free
Facilities: Café, restaurant. Toilets and baby-changing areas. Museum is wheelchair accessible.
Website: www.museumoflondon.org.uk/docklands

Victoria and Albert Museum of Childhood

This branch of the Victoria and Albert Museum claims to house one of the largest toy collections in the world; it certainly has an impressive array of dolls, dollhouses, stuffed animals, games, trains, puppets, and costumes. Although many exhibits are static do-not-touch displays of toy antiquity, the Museum of Childhood offers interactive areas where visiting children can actually play with toys. Children under age five will enjoy the indoor sandbox and a spot where they can dress in costumes, set up and knock down blocks, and play with dollhouses. There are drop-in activities and a board game–playing area. Because of its location in east London, the Museum of Childhood is out of the way for many tourists, but it is a popular venue for local school groups.

WHERE? WHEN? £?

MUSEUM OF CHILDHOOD

Location: East London, at the corner of Cambridge Heath Road and Old Ford Road
Tube: Bethnal Green station (Central Line)
Address: Cambridge Heath Road, London E2 9PA
Phone/email: 020 8983 5200/mocbookings@vam.ac.uk
Hours: Open daily from 10:00 a.m. to 5:45 p.m. Last admission is 5:30 p.m. Closed December 24–26 and January 1.
Time needed: An hour (longer if attending an activity)
Admission: Free
Facilities: Café (no outside food allowed), outdoor picnic areas (indoor picnic area sometimes available). Toilets and baby-changing areas. Coat and package check. Museum is wheelchair accessible. Free Wi-Fi throughout museum.
Website: www.museumofchildhood.org.uk

Sherlock Holmes Museum

Are you *sure* that Sherlock Holmes was a fictional character? Using your powers of inductive reasoning, you may have determined that Mr. Holmes is indeed a fake. This museum is a fake, too—an elaborate, fun, and almost believable fake filled with Sherlock Holmes memorabilia. In the famous detective's study, kids can put on a deerstalker hat, pick up a meerschaum pipe, and utter the inevitable "Elementary, my dear Watson" to their hearts' content.

Rejuvenated interest in the world's most famous fictional detective—literature, movies, and television series—is good news for anyone looking for a Sherlock experience in London. If you emerge from the museum seeking more landmarks for this enduring character, check out some other London locations.

Look for the Sherlock Holmes motif on the walls of Baker Street Underground station. The nine-foot-high bronze statue of the detective standing outside the station is hard to miss. Speedy's Café, the sandwich shop frequented by Holmes and Watson in the BBC's *Sherlock* series, is a real café on Gower Street, near Euston rail station. In the series, the Gower Street location is the stand-in for 221b Baker Street. The café serves up Sherlock-themed snacks.

The Sherlock Holmes pub is a short walk from Charing Cross Underground and rail stations. This is where Holmes tracked down Francis Hay Moulton in *The Noble Bachelors*. Inside the pub there's a replica of Holmes' study, Sherlock memorabilia, and Dr. Watson's old service revolver. Other literary locations and favorite Holmes haunts include the British Museum, Royal Opera House, and the Lyceum Theatre.

WHERE? WHEN? £?

SHERLOCK HOLMES MUSEUM

Location: Near the southwest corner of Regent's Park

Tube: Baker Street station (Bakerloo, Jubilee, Metropolitan, or Circle Line)

Address: 221b Baker Street, London NW1 6XE

Phone/email: 020 7224 3688/ curator@sherlock-holmes.co.uk

Hours: Open daily from 9:30 a.m. to 6:00 p.m. Closed December 25.

Time needed: Thirty to forty-five minutes

Admission: Tickets are reasonably priced, and there are discounts for children. At busy times buy tickets first from the museum shop before getting in line.

Facilities: Toilets on-site. Most areas of the museum are not wheelchair accessible.

Website: www.sherlock-holmes.co.uk

An Art Museum or Two

For many kids, visiting art museums is challenging at best. But some budding artists are fascinated by art museums. You know your children best—for families who want to include an art stop or two, London offers a wealth of choices. Two of the finest are the Tate Modern and the National Gallery.

Tate Modern

It's worth a visit to the Tate Modern just to see the building. This former power plant sits on the bank of the Thames at the south end of the Millennium Bridge. The scale of the building is awe-inspiring. Visitors feel dwarfed in the huge turbine room, which once housed massive electrical-generating equipment. Each year, the museum commissions an artist to install artwork in this space; given the size of the area, the displays are often impressive simply because of their scale.

The Tate offers a dedicated welcome room for families, and there's an open studio where kids can take part in artistic activities. These areas are open on weekends and on Thursdays and Fridays during holiday periods. Many children will enjoy the interactive digital drawing area in the museum.

Families can rent a multimedia guide at the Tate Modern to use while touring the museum. The Tate's website has downloadable game apps that turn museum visits into hunt-and-seek adventures. The museum offers special programs for older children (check the Tate's website for schedules). The Tate Modern's café and restaurant offer welcome respite after touring the galleries. Even more welcome—on most days at lunchtime children age twelve and under eat free.

The Tate Modern's expansion, scheduled to be completed in 2016, incorporates more exhibit spaces, a dedicated children's gallery, and an additional entrance on the south side of the museum complex.

WHERE? WHEN? £?

TATE MODERN

Location: On the south bank of the Thames, near the Millennium Bridge and the Globe Theatre

Tube: Southwark (Jubilee Line)

Address: Bankside, London SE1 9TG

Phone/email: 020 7887 8888/
visiting.modern@tate.org.uk

Hours: Open daily from 10:00 a.m. to 6:00 p.m. Open Friday and Saturday until 10:00 p.m. Closed December 24–26.

Time needed: An hour with younger kids in tow; longer if patience allows

Admission: Free, except for special exhibits

Facilities: Café and restaurant. Toilets and baby-changing area/nursing room. Museum is wheelchair accessible.

Website: www.tate.org.uk (select "Tate Modern")

National Gallery

Overlooking busy Trafalgar Square, Britain's National Gallery has a permanent collection that spans the art universe from the mid-1400s to 1900. There are iconic paintings here, such as one of Van Gogh's *Sunflowers* and a number of works by Britain's own J. M. W. Turner. The National Gallery's collection is so vast—more than 2,300 masterpieces on public display—that visiting families may want to consider taking one of the museum's highlights tours, such as "Impressionism and Beyond," featuring five key artists. The gallery also offers family-oriented audio tours and printed trail guides.

The National Gallery's education center, located on Orange Street at the rear of the building, offers baby-changing areas, toilets, and a street-level entryway into the site. On weekends and during holidays, families can check coats and other items here. Most family-oriented special events are held in the education center.

WHERE? WHEN? £?

NATIONAL GALLERY

Location: Trafalgar Square
Tube: Charing Cross station (Northern or Bakerloo Line) or Leicester Square (Northern or Piccadilly Line)
Address: Trafalgar Square, London WC2N 5DN
Phone/email: 020 7747 2885/ information@ng-london.org.uk
Hours: Open daily from 10:00 a.m. to 6:00 p.m. Open Friday until 9:00 p.m. Closed December 24–26 and January 1.
Time needed: An hour with young children; longer if patience allows
Admission: Free

Facilities: Café and restaurant. Picnic lunches are allowed in the education center and in the foyer outside the Gallery's Sainsbury Wing. Toilets and baby-changing areas/nursing room. Most areas of the museum are wheelchair accessible.

Website: www.nationalgallery.org.uk

Fountain at Trafalgar Square and the National Gallery

Fun, but Perhaps a Tad Tacky

L ondon is full of historic sites, top-notch museums, and cultural icons. But not every venue falls squarely into one of these categories. The city has its share of tacky, kitschy, and lowbrow attractions.

Madame Tussaud's Wax Museum — Gee, Don't They Look Lifelike?

Not everyone is a fan of wax museums. There's something weird and macabre about these worlds of wax. After all, Madame Tussaud began her career by displaying the death masks of people executed during the French Revolution. Fortunately, visitors to Madame Tussaud's have the option to skip scary parts. If you want to bypass the dripping, disgusting chamber of horrors and stick to entertainers, sports figures, and famous folks, just follow the signs.

Wax figures are lifelike, but they lack certain human qualities, such as mortality and ego, so the museum can create some combinations that would be improbable in real life. There's nothing to prevent Michael Jackson from communing with Gandhi, or Albert Einstein from kibitzing with Madonna. To our knowledge, the museum has yet to display those unlikely combinations, but at one time Madame Tussaud's enabled King Henry VIII to gather all his wives together in one room without anyone losing her head. E. T. is here, too (guess he preferred life in London to returning home). Children visiting from abroad will recognize many of the figures in the Wax Museum, but perhaps not every British football star or politician.

Wax Museum visitors can climb into the shell of a London taxi and take a brief ride highlighting the city's history. In a couple of minutes, you are whisked past the Great Fire, the building of St. Paul's, the Victorian era, the Blitz, and back to present-day London. Good news—no taxi driver, so no tip is required.

Madame Tussaud's is one of the most visited attractions in London. Lines to get in are often long, but they move fairly fast. Because it is more than 200 years old, Madame Tussaud's almost qualifies as a historic site itself, albeit a very commercial one.

WHERE? WHEN? £?

MADAME TUSSAUD'S WAX MUSEUM

Location: South of Regent's Park, just down the street from the Sherlock Holmes Museum

Tube: Baker Street station (Circle, Bakerloo, Jubilee, or Metropolitan Line)

Address: Marylebone Road, London NW1 5LR

Phone/email: 0871 894 3000/ guest.experience@madame-tussauds.com

Hours: Hours vary by season. Closed December 25.

Time needed: One to two hours

Admission: Tickets are very expensive. There are discounts for children, seniors, and families. Late-afternoon admission is marginally less expensive. Priority tickets are available for an extra fee. Tickets booked online are less pricey than same-day tickets purchased at the site.

Facilities: Coffee shop on-site. Toilets available. Stroller/buggy storage area available. Most areas are wheelchair accessible.

Website: www.madametussauds.com/london

London Dungeon — Tackiness and Terror

The London Dungeon has always been scary, gory, fun, and macabre . . . pick your adjective. The dungeon moved in 2013, allowing the operators to boast about a newer, bigger, bolder, and better attraction. While "bolder and better" is subjective, the dungeon is certainly newer and bigger at its current site near the London Eye.

Parents traveling with young children should be aware that some exhibits, especially wax museums, dungeons, and the like, are designed to frighten the daylights out of most kids and many adults. Madame Tussaud's is an offender; the London Dungeon is one of the worst. To give you an idea of just how perverse the London Dungeon is, here's a description taken from an old visitor's guide:

> Exhibition depicting the darker side of British Medieval History, Death, Torture, Damnation and Disease. The dark, slimy vaults contain Trials by Ordeal, History of Capital Punishment and the Tortures used in the Tower of London. . . . A major attraction is The Jack the Ripper Experience—a 20 min multi-media exhibition throughout the year. Also on display are the "headcrushers" from France and the Spanish "garrotters."

Need we say more? To see real dungeons, head for the Tower of London.

WHERE? WHEN? £?

LONDON DUNGEON

Location: County Hall building next to the London Eye
Tube: Waterloo station (Bakerloo, Jubilee, Northern, or Waterloo & City Line) or Westminster station (Circle, District, or Jubilee Line) with a scenic walk across Westminster Bridge

Address: County Hall, Westminster Bridge Road, London SE1 7PB

Phone/email: 0871 423 2240 (UK calls only)/ LDGuestExperience@merlinentertainments.biz

Hours: Hours vary by season and during holiday periods. Closed December 25.

Time needed: Ninety minutes (less if you run out screaming sooner)

Admission: Tickets are expensive, but there are discounts for children and seniors. Lowest-priced tickets are available online. Combination tickets for nearby aquarium and London Eye also available.

Facilities: Toilets on-site (and that's a *good* thing). Most areas are wheelchair accessible. Some rides have health and physical restrictions.

Website: www.thedungeons.com/london

On the River

Britain's maritime history is well represented along the banks of the River Thames by two ships in particular—one that circumnavigated the globe in the sixteenth century and one that fought sea battles in the twentieth century.

HMS Belfast

While standing on Tower Bridge, you can't miss the huge warship anchored just upstream in the Thames. The HMS *Belfast* is a retired World War II cruiser, now open to the public and operated as a floating museum by the Imperial War Museum. The ship saw action in the D-Day invasion and later during the Korean War.

Visiting the *Belfast* is not much different from visiting any one of several retired warships on display in coastal cities elsewhere. But if you're a warship aficionado and you're in the neighborhood, stop by the *Belfast*. Few kids can resist the chance to explore the maze of decks, passageways, and compartments in this old ship.

HMS *Belfast* anchored upstream from Tower Bridge

WHERE? WHEN? £?

HMS *BELFAST*

Location: Floating in the Thames, between London Bridge and Tower Bridge. Enter from a pier in South Bank.

Tube: South bank: London Bridge station (Northern or Jubilee Line)

North bank: Tower Hill station (Circle or District Line), then cross the river on Tower Bridge

Address: The Queen's Walk, London SE1 2JH

Phone: 020 7940 6300

Hours: Open daily March through October from 10:00 a.m. to 6:00 p.m. Closes at 5:00 p.m. from November through February. Last admission is one hour before closing. Closed December 24–26.

Time needed: One to two hours

Admission: Tickets are moderately priced. There are discounts for students and seniors, and children under age sixteen get in free.

Facilities: Café on-site. Toilets available. Some areas are not wheelchair accessible.

Website: www.iwm.org.uk (Click "HMS Belfast")

Golden Hinde II

The *Golden Hinde II* is another nautical tourist attraction along the south bank of the Thames. The *Hinde* is a full-scale reconstruction of the sixteenth-century ship that Sir Francis Drake sailed around the world. The ship is moored at St. Mary Overie Dock, just up the river from London Bridge. Like the original, the new *Golden Hinde* sailed around the world, but the modern ship started its journey in California in 1973.

History buffs will appreciate the ship because Sir Francis Drake's accomplishments personify the height of British sea power; children may wish to stop here just to check out the ship. Those who want to get more in touch with the salty life of tall-ship sailing can arrange to spend the night on board during one of the *Golden Hinde*'s occasional living-history events. Berths are on the hard wooden lower decks, so bring a pillow!

If you are in the area, consider walking just a bit farther to Southwark Cathedral (cathedral.southwark.anglican.org). Although it is little known to tourists, this is one of the finest medieval churches in London. Local resident John Harvard was baptized in the cathedral in 1607—he went on to found Harvard University. Don't miss the memorial to William Shakespeare, who reclines below a stained glass window depicting characters from many of his plays.

Other Southwark residents leaned more toward infamy than fame; the area was once filled with brothels, prisons, and other seedy elements. Nearby Clink Prison exhibit (www.clink.co.uk) is *not* a recommended family attraction because, like the London Dungeon, its so-called hands-on educational experience highlights torture and mayhem.

WHERE? WHEN? £?

GOLDEN HINDE II

Location: On the south bank of the Thames, just upstream from London Bridge

Tube: London Bridge (Jubilee or Northern Line) or Monument station (Circle or District Line), then walk across London Bridge

Address: St. Mary Overie Dock, Cathedral Street, London SE1 9DE

Phone/email: 020 7403 0123/info@goldenhinde.com

Hours: Open daily from 10:00 a.m. to 5:30 p.m. Call to confirm opening times.

Time needed: Thirty minutes to an hour. Longer for special events.

Admission: Tickets are reasonably priced. There are discounts for children, families, and seniors.

Website: www.goldenhinde.com

The *Golden Hinde II* sleeps at its mooring.

PART TWO

Hey Kids! Let's...

Go to the Park
Go Cruisin'
Do a Brass Rubbing
Go Shopping
Go to the Theater
Start Ramblin'
Find the Wild Kingdom
Watch the Changing of the Guard
Go for the Gold
Go down the River
Go up the River

Go to the Park

I want always to be a little boy and to have fun.
So I ran away to Kensington Gardens
and lived a long long time among the fairies.
—*Peter Pan*, by J. M. Barrie

London has some of the most beautiful parks and some of the most awesome playgrounds in the world. Stroll through them as a family and everyone is happy; adults can admire English gardening miracles while children run and play. Never underestimate the value of simply sitting on a park bench and soaking up the atmosphere of London (unless it is raining—that's not the "atmosphere" you'll want to soak up). In warm weather, lawn chairs are spread across London's expansive parks. A word of caution: if you sit down in a lawn chair, you've rented that chair. To relax for free, sit on a park bench or a picnic cloth.

While parents may plan a sophisticated, expensive overseas trip, sometimes their children would just as soon stay home. Because you are reading this book, you may have already chosen to ignore this truth. You are sure that a visit to London will be a fun, educational, horizon-broadening experience for the whole family. You're absolutely correct, but don't rule out letting your kids explore London's playgrounds and parks as part of the trip.

For visitors with young children, playgrounds serve two purposes. First, they are a good break from an intense schedule of sightseeing. Forced to behave themselves in hotels, restaurants, cathedrals, theaters, and museums, most kids can stand to burn off some energy on a playground. The second purpose of playgrounds is simple bribery. You might be able to get through that last museum gallery if you bribe your kids with the promise of a playground break. Fortunately, visitors don't have to look far for a playground in London because they're located in big parks and shoehorned into tiny lots between buildings.

St. James's Park and Green Park

St. James's Park tops our list as the most beautiful park in central London. Situated between Buckingham Palace and the government offices at Whitehall, St. James's is an island of green surrounded by many of London's prime historic sites. In 1827, John Nash designed the park that visitors see today, but this space has been a royal park since King Henry VIII acquired St. James's in the early sixteenth century.

There's only one playground here, and walking on the grass is not allowed in some areas, but St. James's Park is a great place to take children. Before your trip, watch the movie *101 Dalmatians* (the live-action version starring Glenn Close, not the animated film). St. James's Park is the site of the frantic bicycle chase scene that ends when Pongo and Perdita's human masters land in the park's lake. In this same lake, kids can spot pelicans, flamingos,

Bird keeper's cottage, St. James's Park

and swans—some of the twenty species of waterfowl that live in the park. Look for the shy, rare black swans at the island nearest Whitehall, hiding beneath overhanging tree branches. All the birds gather around when the pelicans are fed by the park staff at about 2:30 p.m.

Green Park is just across the street from St. James's Park, and until recently it was known as Upper St. James's Park. Because Green Park dates to the 1500s, "recently" refers to the mid-1700s. Once used as a dueling ground, Green Park is now another pleasant spot with tall trees and broad lawns serving as a serene buffer between the palace and Mayfair's busy Piccadilly thoroughfare.

The flowery grounds of St. James's Park are beautiful to look at, while Green Park is a prime spot to rent a lawn chair and relax. The parks are not all nature and quiet gardens, though. St. James's hosts band concerts in the summer. And the peace and quiet are truly shattered when artillery gun salutes are fired from one of the parks to celebrate a royal birthday or other occasion.

WHERE? WHEN? £?

ST. JAMES'S PARK AND GREEN PARK

Location: St. James's Park is between Buckingham Palace and Horse Guards Parade. Green Park is just north of St. James's Park, close to Buckingham Palace.

Tube: St. James's Park station (Circle or District Line); Green Park station (Jubilee, Victoria, or Piccadilly Line)

Address: The St. James's Park Office, The Storeyard, St. James's Park, Horse Guards Parade, London SW1A 2BJ

Phone/Email: 030 0061 2350/ stjames@royalparks.gsi.gov.uk

Hours: St. James's Park is open from 5:00 a.m. to midnight. Green Park is always open.

Time needed: You can speed through in thirty minutes, stroll for an hour, or spend an afternoon relaxing here.

Admission: Free
Facilities: Cafés and restaurant, plenty of picnic opportunities. Toilets in Green Park are at the northeast corner near the Green Park Tube station. In St. James's Park, toilets are at the east end near Horse Guards Parade and in the center at Marlborough Gate.
Website: www.royalparks.gov.uk

Hyde Park and Kensington Gardens

Hyde Park, along with adjoining Kensington Gardens, is a massive expanse of green in the core of London. Hyde Park dates to the early 1500s, when it was a royal hunting ground. The park packs a wealth of activities kids will enjoy:

- Boating and fishing on the Serpentine lake
- Seasonal swimming from the Lido
- Tennis, lawn bowling, and putting greens
- Biking and horseback riding
- Playgrounds
- Concerts
- Environmental learning at the LookOut Education Centre

Boating on Hyde Park's Serpentine is a favorite good-weather activity. A solar-powered shuttle boat silently whisks passengers across the Serpentine; the unique craft operates (weather permitting) on weekends in March, April, May, and September and daily in June, July, and August. Visitors can also rent canoes and paddleboats from Hyde Park's boathouse.

We've noted that St. James's Park was a playground for Dalmatians Pongo and Perdita. Nearby Kensington Gardens has its own story for children: Peter Pan lived here. He's still here, in fact, and kids will enjoy discovering the Peter Pan sculpture in

Kensington Gardens. Don't get too excited; it is just a statue, but if you *believe* . . .

The search for Peter Pan and his pirates draws long lines of London children to Kensington Gardens, where a popular playground evokes the memory of two of Kensington's most famous residents: the unlikely pair of Princess Diana and Peter Pan. The Diana Princess of Wales Memorial Playground is on the site of an earlier playground donated by *Peter Pan* author J. M. Barrie. Kensington Palace was Diana's official home, and the princess often sought anonymous refuge in Kensington Gardens.

But it's the playground, not the memorial or literary connections, that attracts kids. A fully rigged pirate ship seemingly grounded on a beach dominates the two-acre site. Children can climb a hidden passage between the galleon's three decks and even try to refloat the ship by moving sand out of the ballast. The park's beach cove (watch out for the crocodiles!) is a water play area where kids can search for the imprints of fossils and even a mermaid's tail. When children tire of the pirate ship and cove, they can move on to the tree house camp and call each other using the park's "tree-phones." Then it's on to the Native American

Ahoy! Pirate ships in Kensington Gardens

teepees, or maybe a stop in the Movement and Musical Garden to make music, or at least joyful noise. The Peter Pan theme continues in the park's restroom facilities, located in the Home under the Ground. Can't quite recall Peter Pan's story? Home under the Ground is where the Lost Boys lived.

Kensington Gardens is essentially a western extension of Hyde Park. Together, the two parks form a green oasis stretching from the backyard of Buckingham Palace all the way to Kensington Palace. Other highlights here are the gardens around Kensington Palace, a model boat pond, a seasonal restaurant, areas for kite flying, and a puppet theater.

The Diana Memorial Fountain is located just south of the Serpentine Bridge in Hyde Park and is one of the most visited areas of any park in London. The Diana Memorial is low-key, as royal monuments go; contrast it with the nearby ornate Albert Memorial, erected by Queen Victoria to honor her beloved husband, Prince Albert. There's a sobering memorial near the southeast corner of Hyde Park. The fifty-two stark steel pillars are dedicated to the Londoners who lost their lives in the city's July 7, 2005, terrorist bombings.

During the summer, Hyde Park often hosts rock concerts and other huge events. It pays to check the park's events listings if you want to attend an event or avoid the crowds.

Young equestrians and their parents can gain a different perspective on Hyde Park by signing up for a ride at Hyde Park Stables (www.hydeparkstables.com). Five miles of trails wind through the park, allowing visitors to combine horseback riding with sightseeing. There is a weight limit of 175 pounds for horseback riding, and the stables provide riding helmets. No previous riding experience is required, and children over age five are welcome. However, the cost of a horseback ride through the park is expensive. A better alternative? Rent a bicycle from London's nearby cycle hire stations and ride along several designated bike routes in the parks.

WHERE? WHEN? £?

HYDE PARK AND KENSINGTON GARDENS

Location: West of Mayfair and north of Kensington, stretching from the end of Buckingham Palace gardens all the way to Kensington Palace

Tube: The area is ringed by Tube stops. For Kensington Palace, use High Street Kensington station (Circle or District Line) on the south or Queensway station (Central Line) on the north. Other stations along the north border of the park are Lancaster Gate and Marble Arch (both on the Central Line). Stations along the south are Hyde Park Corner and Knightsbridge (both on the Piccadilly Line).

Address: Hyde Park Office, Rangers Lodge, Hyde Park, London W2 2UH; Kensington Gardens Office, Magazine Store Yard, Magazine Gate, Kensington Gardens, London W2 2UH

Phone/email: 030 0061 2000/hyde@royalparks.gsi .gov.uk; kensington@royalparks.gsi.gov.uk

Hours: Most areas are open from 5:00 a.m. until midnight, but the gardens around the palace are open from 6:00 a.m. to dusk. The Diana Memorial Fountain opens at 10:00 a.m.; the closing time varies depending on the time of year.

Time needed: This green area is almost two miles long, so seeing all of it will take a while. Spend an hour or an afternoon.

Admission: Free

Facilities: Cafés, restaurants, snack bars, and plenty of picnic spots. Toilets in several locations. Most areas of the parks are wheelchair accessible and there is a shuttle service for the mobility impaired.

Websites: www.royalparks.gov.uk; www.solarshuttle.co.uk (boating); www.supporttheroyalparks.org (education center)

Where? When? £?

Diana Memorial Playground

Location: In the northwest corner of Kensington Gardens, near Kensington Palace

Tube: Queensway station (Central Line)

Phone/email: 030 0061 2001/ dianaplayground@royalparks.gsi.gov.uk .

Hours: The playground is open to children age twelve and under. Unaccompanied adults may tour the playground from 9:30 a.m. to 10:00 a.m. only. The playground opens at 10:00 a.m.; the closing time varies depending on the time of year. Last admission is fifteen minutes before closing. Closed December 25. During crowded periods, expect a line to get in.

Time needed: Who's asking? Kids may not want to leave at all.

Cost: Free

Facilities: Café. Toilets and baby-changing areas.

Website: www.royalparks.gov.uk

Coram's Fields

Not far from the British Museum, a seven-acre play area sits, appropriately enough, on the site of one of London's first charities to help children. The Foundling Hospital is long gone, although the nearby Foundling Museum is worth a visit (www.foundlingmuseum.org.uk). In the hospital's place is Coram's Fields—a large park incorporating playgrounds, a community center, and a small city farm. Many of the activities here are geared to local residents, but visiting children are welcome to explore. The park is open only to children under age sixteen (adults without children are not allowed). The children's center and the youth center (for ages thirteen to nineteen) offer drop-in activities.

Where? When? £?

Coram's Fields

Location: Near Russell Square and the British Museum
Tube: Russell Square (Piccadilly Line)
Address: 93 Guilford Street, London WC1N 1DN
Phone: 020 7837 6138
Hours: 9:00 a.m. to dusk
Time needed: An hour (longer if attending an activity)
Admission: Free
Facilities: Cafés. Toilets in several locations.
Website: www.coramsfields.org

Regent's Park

The largest park in downtown London is located on the northern border of the city center. Regent's Park, like many others, began its life as royal hunting grounds during the reign of Henry VIII. The park was landscaped by John Nash in the early 1800s.

There's a little of everything here. Regent's Park is sports oriented, with a running track, athletic fields, and—surprisingly—American softball. A stroll north lands you at the London Zoo. During warm months, the scent of roses wafts from Queen Mary's Garden in the center of the park. In the summer, Regent's Park hosts an open-air theater featuring Shakespeare and other popular productions. There is also a children's boating pond where kids can captain small paddleboats. And yes, Regent's Park has playgrounds (four of them).

Where? When? £?

Regent's Park

Location: North of the Marylebone area and less than a mile northwest of Hyde Park

Tube: Baker Street station (Circle, Bakerloo, Jubilee, or Metropolitan Line) or Regent's Park station (Bakerloo Line)

Address: Regent's Park Office, The Store Yard, Inner Circle, Regent's Park, London NW1 4NR

Phone/email: 030 0061 2300/ regents@royalparks.gsi.gov.uk

Hours: 5:00 a.m. to dusk

Time needed: Whatever you wish

Admission: Free

Facilities: Cafés, restaurants, snack bars, and plenty of picnic spots. Toilets in several locations. Most areas of the park are wheelchair accessible.

Website: www.royalparks.gov.uk; www.openairtheatre.com (theater)

Hampstead Heath

Let's go fly a kite
Up to the highest height!
Let's go fly a kite and send it soaring
Up through the atmosphere
Up where the air is clear
Oh, let's go fly a kite!

—*Mary Poppins*, words and music by
Richard M. Sherman and Robert B. Sherman

Hampstead Heath is an oasis of open space just four miles from the hustle and bustle of central London. Hampstead, the village that adjoins the heath, is an upscale neighborhood featuring some of London's most expensive residential real estate.

Visiting the 790-acre heath is like stepping through a portal into the green countryside of England. You can *see* London—the views of the city are incredible—but you can barely hear it. The sounds of Hampstead Heath are more likely to be those of a summertime concert on the grounds of historic Kenwood House, joggers puffing their way along pathways, or the squeal of kite-flying children.

Did we say kite flying? The musical *Mary Poppins* concludes with the once-troubled Banks family happily flying a kite in Hampstead (or a least the Hollywood sound stage version). Another Poppins-related site in Hampstead is the Admiral's House, where fictional Admiral Boom fires a cannon from his rooftop every day. Mary Shepard, illustrator of the original Mary Poppins book series, lived in Hampstead and took many inspirations from the area, as did author P. L. Travers.

Hampstead Heath offers swimming and fishing ponds, playgrounds, bandstands, and even a small zoo. If your children want to fly a kite, or just run off some pent-up energy, Hampstead Heath is the perfect spot.

WHERE? WHEN? £?

HAMPSTEAD HEATH

Location: In the borough of Camden, about four miles north of central London

Tube: Three Northern Line stations serve the area: Golders Green station in the northern portion of the park, Hampstead station in the southwest, and Kentish Town station to the southeast.

Phone/email: 020 7332 3322/ hampstead.heath@cityoflondon.gov.uk

Hours: Portions open at 7:30 a.m. or 8:30 a.m. until dusk, but most of the heath is always open.
Time needed: Several hours or longer
Admission: Free
Facilities: Cafés at Parliament Hill and Golders Hill, and restaurant at Kenwood House. Public toilets in various locations. Many areas of Hampstead Heath are wheelchair accessible.
Website: www.cityoflondon.gov.uk/hampsteadheath

Visit the Park after Dark?

In England, there was scarcely an amount of order and protection to justify much national boasting. Daring burglaries by armed men, and highway robberies, took place in the capital itself every night.
—*A Tale of Two Cities*, by Charles Dickens

Based on Charles Dickens's description, London street crime was a real problem in 1775. Although today's streetwise travelers generally avoid city parks after dark, London's central parks still feel relatively safe, even at night. Crime exists in London, but violent street crime is not common. The most threatening sights we've seen during evening walks in St. James's and Green Parks were the guards on patrol near a royal residence; we rounded a corner and faced two camouflaged soldiers carrying automatic weapons! Although many parks officially close in the evenings, their pathways are used by late-night urban strollers. Normal precautions apply.

Go Cruisin'

Believe me, my young friend, there is nothing—absolutely nothing—half
so much worth doing as simply messing about in boats.
—*The Wind in the Willows*, by Kenneth Grahame

This section is devoted to cruising in London. Because this is
a family travel publication, we define cruising in a family-
friendly way: riverboat cruises on the Thames, a unique amphibious tour on the river *and* through town, canal boat cruises on
Regent's Canal, and a cruise (actually more of a "spin") on the
London Eye.

River Cruises

Taking a boat ride in London can serve many purposes:

- The water view provides a unique perspective on many of
  London's famous sites.
- Sometimes a boat is the most practical way to get to where
  you're going.
- The phrase "Hey, kids, let's go on a boat trip!" is usually
  received with more enthusiasm than "Hey, kids, let's go
  into this cathedral!"

Boating on the Thames is a practical and fun way to reach
several destinations from central London: downriver to Greenwich,
Canary Wharf, and the Thames River flood barrier; upriver to
Richmond, Kew, and Hampton Court; or just sightseeing between
Tower Bridge and Westminster. Transport for London operates
or coordinates most river services. There has been a concerted
effort to expand the use of the Thames by commuters as well as
pleasure cruisers, and the Transport for London website lists a
dizzying array of boat routes.

Before taking a cruise to someplace like Hampton Court, decide how much time you want to spend on a boat (Hampton is a four-hour boat ride from London). The Thames loops and turns, so river trips can take much longer than other modes of transportation. On a more manageable scale, visitors can take fifty-minute evening sightseeing cruises from several London river piers. If the weather is nice, this is a relaxing, low-key evening activity. And sunset on the Thames can be magnificent.

WHERE? WHEN? £?

THAMES RIVER CRUISES

Location: London has a number of river piers, but many popular cruises leave from Westminster Pier (just downstream from Big Ben), Tower Pier (near the Tower of London), and Embankment Pier.

Tube: Westminster Pier: Westminster station (Circle or District Line); Tower Pier: Tower Hill station (Circle or District Line); Embankment Pier: Charing Cross station (Bakerloo or Northern Line)

Time needed: The sightseeing boat from Westminster Pier to Tower Pier takes about twenty minutes; a boat from London to Greenwich takes about an hour; Hampton Court is almost four hours up the river from London.

Fares: Fares range widely. The least expensive are short jaunts on commuter boat routes; the most expensive are evening cruises featuring (often mediocre) champagne, food, and entertainment. Some discounts are available if you have a Transport for London Oyster card.

Facilities: Larger boats have food concessions, toilets, and other facilities. Most boats are wheelchair accessible.

Website: www.tfl.gov.uk (look for the "River" section). The site also links to individual commercial boat operators.

Hop aboard the Duck

Can't decide whether to take a bus tour on London's streets or a boat tour on the Thames? You can do both on board a DUKW. These craft started out as World War II amphibious vehicles, capable of wading through rivers and driving overland. Refitted and painted bright yellow, these strange-looking hybrids take visitors on a land-and-water tour through central London before splashing down into the Thames and returning to the London Eye.

Yes, the bright yellow DUKWS look out of place (some would say tacky) rumbling past Big Ben. But that won't faze most children. The Duck Tour is a big hit with many visiting families.

Quack! Duck Tour on the Thames

Where? When? £?

Duck Tours

Location: Between Waterloo rail station and the London Eye, on the south bank of the Thames
Tube: Waterloo station (Bakerloo, Jubilee, Northern, or Waterloo & City Line)
Address: Departure point: Chicheley Street, London SE1 7PY; Offices: London Duck Tours Limited, 55 York Road, London SE1 7NJ
Phone/email: 020 7928 3132/ enquiries@londonducktours.co.uk
Hours: 9:00 a.m. to 6:00 p.m. Hours vary by season. Closed December 24–26 and 31 and January 1.
Time needed: Seventy-five minutes
Admission: Tickets are expensive, but there are discounts for children, families, students, and seniors. Tickets can be booked online.
Facilities: No onboard facilities. Not wheelchair accessible.
Website: www.londonducktours.co.uk

Canal Boats

There's no better way to get to the London Zoo than to cruise on a boat up or down Regent's Canal. Of course, you don't have to stop and see the animals at the zoo; canal cruises are a great way to relax and get off the beaten path. Walking the canal towpath is also possible; there are a few interesting regency buildings, iron bridges, and tunnels along the way. London's canals connected the city's manufacturing centers before railways took over.

At one end of a Regent's Canal boat trip is Little Venice, home to waterside cafés, pubs, and eateries. Camden Town, at the other end of the boat trip, is best known for its alternative culture, international markets, and music venues.

The London Waterbus operates one way or roundtrip service between Camden Lock and Little Venice, and between these points and the London Zoo. Jason's Trips provides a roundtrip sightseeing cruise starting at Little Venice. The Jenny Wren sightseeing round-trips start and end near Camden Lock.

WHERE? WHEN? £?

REGENT'S CANAL BOAT TRIPS

Location: This portion of Regent's Canal runs from Little Venice (just north of Paddington rail station) around the top of Regent's Park to Camden Lock (east of the park).

Tube: Little Venice: Warwick Avenue station (Bakerloo Line); Camden Lock: Camden Town station (Northern Line)

Address: Jason's Trips: Opposite 42 Blomfield Road, London W9; London Waterbus: 58 Camden Lock Place, London NW1 8AF; Jenny Wren: Walkers Quay, 250 Camden High Street, London NW1 8QS

Phone/email: Jason's Trips: 020 7286 3248/ info@jasons.co.uk
London Waterbus Company: 020 7482 2550/ canaltrips@londonwaterbus.com/
Jenny Wren: 020 7485 4433/info@walkersquay.com

Hours: Boats operate full schedules from April through October. London Waterbus operates limited service in other months.

Time needed: About ninety minutes round-trip from Little Venice to Camden Lock

Admission: Tickets are inexpensive. There are discounts for children, seniors, and families.

Facilities: Toilets at docking points and onboard the Jenny Wren. Limited wheelchair accessibility.
Websites: www.jasons.co.uk; www.londonwaterbus .com; www.walkersquay.com (Jenny Wren)

The London Eye

My favorite thing to do in London is to fly the Eye. . . .
On a clear day you can see for twenty-five miles in all directions. . . . It takes thirty minutes to go full circle.
And then your capsule goes lower and you are sad because you do not want the ride to end. You would like to go round one more time, but it's not allowed.
So you get out feeling like an astronaut coming down from space, a little lighter than you were.
—*The London Eye Mystery,* by Siobhan Dowd

It's hard to miss the giant Ferris wheel across the river from Big Ben and Parliament. The London Eye's operators insist that their commercial venture is an "observation wheel," not a Ferris wheel, but that is a distinction most visitors miss.

Terminology aside, the London Eye is a fantastic vantage point from which to view downtown London. Visitors ride in large observation pods that slowly rotate around the 450-foot-tall wheel. The combination of the slow motion and the enclosed pods makes for a tame ride. Visibility is up to twenty-five miles, so on a clear day you can't see forever, but you might see as far as the town of Windsor. Riding the London Eye at sunset on a clear or partly cloudy day is an unforgettable London experience.

During busy summer months, lines can be long at this popular attraction. Advance booking is a good idea.

Dizzy? Don't look down from the London Eye

WHERE? WHEN? £?

THE LONDON EYE

Location: On the south bank of the Thames, just downstream from Parliament and next to County Hall

Tube: Waterloo station (Bakerloo, Jubilee, Northern, or Waterloo & City Line); also Embankment station (Bakerloo, Circle, District, or Northern Line) or Westminster station (Circle or District Line), then walk across Westminster Bridge

Address: Riverside Building, County Hall, Westminster Bridge Road, London SE1 7PB

Phone/email: 0870 990 8883 (UK calls only)/ customer.services@londoneye.com

Hours: Opens at 10:00 a.m. Closes at 8:30 p.m. in September through early April. Stays open later in spring and summer months, but schedule varies, so check the website. Closed December 25 and generally closed for one week each January.

Time needed: Thirty minutes for the ride, plus waiting time

Admission: General admission tickets are moderately priced; priority entry tickets are expensive. There are discounts for children and seniors, and kids under age four ride free. Tickets can be booked online.

Facilities: Cafés available on-site. Toilets and baby-changing areas. Fully wheelchair accessible.

Website: www.londoneye.com

Do a Brass Rubbing

If the weather turns nasty during a visit to London (and it may), doing a brass rubbing is a fun rainy-day activity for families. The tradition started with rubbings on the ancient burial vault brasses of knights and nobility, done on paper using chalk or charcoal. Eventually, all that rubbing began to threaten the survival of the brasses, so copies were cast. Brass rubbing centers have large selections of brass casts; kids can choose to copy knights, ladies, dragons, or other medieval brasses.

Here's the process. Start by taping a large piece of rubbing paper to the face of the brass plate, then carefully rub across the paper with a special colored rubbing crayon. It's similar to putting a piece of paper on top of a coin and rubbing it with a pencil. Seemingly endless rubbing with the crayon produces a two-dimensional copy of the brass. The rubbing center staff will roll up the completed work and place it in a cardboard mailing tube. When you get home, frame the brass rubbing. The best thing about this souvenir is that you made it yourself!

Brass rubbing is a good activity for artistically inclined children from about age seven and up. It takes a while to satisfactorily complete a brass rubbing, so plan at least thirty minutes to an hour or more, depending on your skill, persistence, and the size of the brass on which you are working.

There is a brass rubbing center at St. Martin-in-the-Fields Church just off Trafalgar Square.

St. Martin's has a cafeteria where hungry brass rubbers can get a quick meal. The caf-

Brass rubbing fun

eteria floor is partially made of stone slabs that mark the burial places of former church members. It's not as macabre as it sounds. After repeated exposure to England's innumerable abbeys, cathedrals, and churches, children become accustomed to walking over the not-so-recently departed. The St. Martin's cafeteria is fast and convenient and provides a lot of reasonably priced choices. While you are here, go upstairs and take a look at the rest of St. Martin-in-the-Fields Church.

St. Martin-in-the-Fields is home to frequent lunchtime musical recitals. These are relatively brief, informal concerts that most children can sit through with minimal squirming. It's a chance for families to absorb some London culture in a palatable dose. The lunchtime concerts are free, but there is a collection bin at the door.

St. Martin's is renowned for its music programs. Adults and older children can enjoy the church's frequent evening candlelight concerts, and St. Martin's crypt is converted into an atmospheric jazz venue on select Wednesday nights.

WHERE? WHEN? £?

ST. MARTIN-IN-THE-FIELDS BRASS RUBBING CENTRE

Location: Northeast side of Trafalgar Square. If you are facing the church, the entrance pavilion is on the left.

Tube: Charing Cross station (Bakerloo or Northern Line)

Address: The Crypt, St. Martin-in-the-Fields Church, Trafalgar Square, London WC2N 4JJ

Phone/email: 020 7766 1122/shop@smitf.org

Hours: Monday through Wednesday 10:00 a.m. to 6:00 p.m., Thursday through Saturday 10:00 a.m. to 8:00 p.m., Sunday 11:30 a.m. to 5:00 p.m.

Admission: No charge to get in. The cost of brass rubbings depends on their size; a small one costs only a few pounds.

Facilities: Café on-site (no outside food allowed). Toilets and baby-changing areas. Wheelchair accessible.

Website: www.stmartin-in-the-fields.org

St. Martin-in-the-Fields Church

Go Shopping— "Do We Have To?"

Then, one day, James' mother and father went to London to do some shopping, and there a terrible thing happened. Both of them suddenly got eaten up (in full daylight, mind you, and on a crowded street) by an enormous angry rhinoceros which had escaped from the London Zoo.
—*James and the Giant Peach*, by Roald Dahl

Despite the fact that you are unlikely to meet the same fate as James's parents while you are shopping in London, your children may resist the thought of an afternoon in the shops. Arguments against shopping while on vacation are bolstered by several facts:

- London can be an expensive place to shop.
- The value added tax can make things even more expensive.
- You can find much of the same merchandise back home or online.

It's easy to find souvenirs—but you might want to wander off the beaten path for something out of the ordinary

Here's another reason to minimize shopping. You are on vacation in a world-class city, you've spent a lot of money to get here, and London offers all kinds of exciting, unique experiences. So why use valuable vacation time shopping if you can do it just as well at home?

One shopping stop is a must-see for children: Hamley's Toy Store. Hamley's was the top commercial highlight of our kids' first and subsequent visits to London. This is no toy *shop*; Hamley's is a huge, high-quality toy department store on Regent Street. Founded in 1760 and opened in its current location in 1881, Hamley's has seven floors of toys to entice young shoppers and their parents.

WHERE? WHEN? £?

HAMLEY'S TOY STORE

Location: On the east side of Regent Street, a couple of blocks south of Oxford Street and north of Piccadilly Circus

Tube: Oxford Circus station (Central or Victoria Line)

Address: 188–96 Regent Street, London W1B 5BT

Phone/email: 0871 704 1977 (UK calls only)/ customerservices@hamleys.co.uk

Hours: Open Monday through Friday from 10:00 a.m. to 9:00 p.m., Saturday 9:30 a.m. to 9:00 p.m., and Sunday noon to 6:00 p.m. Seasonal and holiday hours vary.

Time needed: Shop till you drop (or go bankrupt)

Facilities: Café on-site. Toilets and baby-changing areas.

Website: www.hamleys.com

Elegant, curving Regent Street is home to a host of major stores. Many are unique to London; some you might find in your hometown. All are expensive. Oxford Street, at the north end of Regent Street, overflows with shopping options, including the large department stores John Lewis, Selfridges, and Marks and Spenser. At times, Oxford Street and Regent Street are wall-to-curb with shopping crowds.

If your philosophy is "I shop, therefore, I am," you won't be disappointed by Harrods in Knightsbridge. But dragging a child through this massive, crowded department store can be torturous. On the plus side, Harrods does have a toy area (although it certainly can't rival Hamley's). Harrods boasts an enormous food hall—walking through this area is a gastronomic event for the whole family. If you pass by Harrods at night, your kids may think that the store is decorated for Christmas because the building is outlined by thousands of tiny lights. Unlike many department stores, Harrods has just two major sales—in July and January—and these events attract throngs of bargain hunters.

By contrast, Fortnum & Mason on Piccadilly Street in Mayfair offers shopping on a scale that most people can handle. The store is impressive; our children remarked that Fortnum & Mason was the only place where they've ever bought cookies from a salesperson wearing a tuxedo. The basement and ground floor food departments are filled with teas, jams, biscuits, and other delicacies. Alas, there's no toy department.

While you're in the Mayfair area, take a walk through Burlington Arcade. You will discover that the shopping mall is not a new phenomenon. The ornate covered arcade off of Piccadilly was built in 1819; it is occupied by a series of upscale shops. Mall security guards here look a little different than those at home. With their top hats and formal uniforms, Burlington Arcade's "beadles" are a combination security guard and information guide. Piccadilly Arcade, right across the street, opened in 1910, so it's a relative retail newcomer. London's prime shopping venues aren't all historic. For example, Australia's Westfield Group has built huge shopping centers in White City (west of Kensington) and at the former Olympic Park in east London.

Another joy of shopping is London's many bookstores, some selling new books and some offering antiquarian tomes. Tourists of all ages will find a wider selection than at home. Children can ditch *Diary of a Wimpy Kid* for *The Adventures of Lupo*, a series starring a royal dog; adults can peruse used bookshops for first editions of great English works (although a first edition of a Dickens novel would be a rather expensive souvenir). A few vintage bookstores survive just north of Trafalgar Square along Charing Cross Road, between Leicester Square and the Tottenham Court Road Tube station. The booksellers are crowded, dusty shops filled floor-to-ceiling with antique books.

London's street markets and traditional food markets offer a glimpse of shopping as it existed before big-box stores and online retail. Depending on their interests and tolerance for browsing, children may enjoy strolling through street markets. London's old-style food markets are also dramatically different from modern grocery stores.

One of the better-known markets consists of antiques and flea market stalls along Portobello Road, best visited on Saturday (Tube stops: Nottinghill Gate or Ladbroke Grove). Portobello

A bit of everything's on sale in Camden

claims to be the world's largest antiques market—perhaps a frightening factoid for visiting children. Camden Market, northeast of Regent's Park, is filled with flea markets and stores offering quirky goods. Camden has open-air market stalls and storefront shops that generally operate seven days a week (Tube stop: Camden Town). For traditional covered food markets, head to restored Leadenhall Market, located in London's financial district (Tube stops: Bank or Monument). Leadenhall is open weekdays from 11:00 a.m. to 4:00 p.m. Greenwich offers an antiques and crafts market (Docklands Light Railway stop: Cutty Sark). This is just a sampling of the many markets scattered throughout London.

Museum shops can provide unique shopping experiences for visitors. The Transport Museum in Covent Garden is filled with souvenirs sporting popular London Transport graphics, and the Tower of London's shops have lots of items for children. While museum shops are not immune to tacky, cheap souvenirs, they do offer books and reproduction items that usually can't be found elsewhere.

The Covent Garden area is filled with specialty shops, especially along Neal Street, just north of the Covent Garden Market. Kids might enjoy stores here that specialize in kites, skates, cartoon art, and toys. There has been a steady trend toward fewer independent shops and more big retailer names in Covent Garden, but the corporate giants have not completely taken over (although the huge Apple store certainly ups the pressure on independent retailers). The small streets and alleyways north and west of the Covent Garden piazza and marketplace continue to house a variety of independent shops. Neal's Yard Dairy, for example, is worth a stop to sample the huge selection of British and European cheeses.

Cheese? Covent Garden's got it

Wherever adults choose to shop in London, they can count on free advice from children:

> "The Toy Department," Michael reminded her, "is in *that* direction."
> "I know thank you. Don't point," [Mary Poppins] said, and paid her bill with aggravating slowness.
> —*Mary Poppins*, by P. L. Travers

Go to the Theater

The theatre was quite full and Paddington waved to the people down below. Much to Mrs. Brown's embarrassment, several of them pointed and waved back.
— *A Bear Called Paddington*, by Michael Bond

London's West End offers a vast array of shows, but finding something appropriate for younger children can be a challenge. Musicals are often a good bet if you choose wisely: *Matilda the Musical*, not *Chicago*; *The Lion King*, not *King Lear*. (OK, *King Lear* isn't a musical, but you get the idea.)

Of course, the Internet is a great resource for choosing shows. The Society of London Theatre's website, www.official londontheatre.co.uk, is, as the name implies, the "official" guide to London theater. The society also operates TKTS, the legitimate discount ticket booth in Leicester Square. The commercial site www.whatsonstage.com has listings for performing arts events throughout Britain. Users can search for events by location, date, or type of performance. Both websites include theater reviews, seating charts, and a way to order tickets, albeit with hefty booking fees. The British branch of Ticketmaster provides a similar online service. After arriving in London, visitors can pick up copies of guides like *Time Out London* for more theater information.

Most of London's major theaters are located in the West End theater district close to Piccadilly Circus or Leicester Square; there's another grouping in the Covent Garden area. Because London's museums and tourist attractions usually close by 6:00 p.m., an evening theater performance works well for many visitors. As a bonus, the theater is a chance to sit down after walking all day. Those who don't mind walking a bit more can use the Tube to get to most theaters, but a taxi will drop you right at the lobby door.

Hailing a taxi after the performance can be a challenge because all shows end at about the same time, and competition for taxis is fierce. The area around Leicester Square, including the Tube stop, is often very crowded with a mixture of theater patrons and a slightly rowdy bar crowd on Friday and Saturday nights, so extra vigilance is advisable when traveling with children.

How to Get Tickets

Ticket agencies in other countries sell London theater tickets, but most charge substantial service fees. Overseas travelers can sometimes order tickets directly from websites or theater box offices. Booking through the box office is often less expensive than using a ticket agent. Keep in mind that many theaters have exclusive marketing deals with commercial ticket agencies that you probably won't be able to bypass.

Other possible sources for theater tickets are airlines, travel agencies, deal-of-the-day websites like Groupon, and ticket agencies in London.

What about discounted theater tickets? Although standing in line at a ticket outlet hardly constitutes family fun, it can save you money. Many tickets are half price plus a small fee. One drawback is that families traveling together need seats together, and these can be hard to find at the bargain outlet. Another problem with the ticket outlet is the limited selection of shows, because the most popular productions don't need to discount tickets. Be wary of using anyplace other than the official TKTS ticket office in Leicester Square. Watch out for ticket touts (scalpers) who ply the Leicester Square area and charge exorbitant rates for sometimes subpar seats.

One obvious way to get tickets is simply to walk up to the theater box office on the day of the show and see what is available. Theaters occasionally have unsold and returned tickets for even popular productions. Finally, if you are desperate to see a popular show and you are staying in an upscale hotel, check with the concierge. A good concierge can sometimes make rare tickets appear as if by magic—for the right price.

Lines for discount tickets in Leicester Square

WHERE? WHEN? £?

TKTS TICKET BOOTH

Location: In the clock tower building on the south side of Leicester Square

Tube: Leicester Square station (Northern or Piccadilly Line)

Phone/email: None

Hours: 10:00 a.m. to 7:00 p.m. Monday through Saturday. Open Sunday from 11:00 a.m. to 4:30 p.m.

Other info: A small fee is added to ticket sales.

Websites: www.tkts.co.uk; www.officiallondontheatre.co.uk

The Globe Theatre

All the world's a stage,
And all the men and women merely players.
—*As You Like It*, by William Shakespeare

Because theater thrives in modern London, it is hard to imagine a time when playwrights and actors struggled against religious and government suppression. But one reason that the Globe Theatre was located on the south bank of the Thames was to escape the unfriendly atmosphere in the city of London. In 1597, after an unsympathetic landlord raised the land rent, the theater company moved the Globe—piece by piece—from its City location to Southwark.

In 1613, the original Globe Theatre burned to the ground, allegedly the result of a cannon shot during a performance of the play *Henry VIII*. A new theater was built on the site, but it lasted only until 1642, when those fun-loving Puritans forced it to close. The Globe was torn down in 1644, and the site was virtually forgotten. It was not until the 1980s that the foundation of the theater was discovered. The remains of the original Globe are buried below a newer (but still historic) building that was constructed on the site.

What Globe visitors see today is a reconstruction begun under the leadership of the late Sam Wanamaker, an American actor and film director. But to call the Globe a reconstruction is to sell it short. The new Globe was painstakingly completed using authentic Elizabethan building techniques, and the result is both a theater and a tourist attraction. In 2014 a new indoor theater opened adjacent to the Globe. The Sam Wanamaker Playhouse is another stunning re-creation—a beautiful 340-seat Jacobean theater. Amazingly, productions in this new space are staged in candlelight.

If your children won't sit still for a full-fledged Shakespearean production on the Elizabethan stage, at least take the building tour of the legendary theater and a quick look at the adjoining Globe Exhibition.

All the world's a stage

Where? When? £?

The Globe Theatre

Location: On the south bank of the Thames, near Southwark Bridge

Tube: Mansion House station (Circle or District Line), then walk across the Millennium Bridge. Alternate is London Bridge station (Northern or Jubilee Line), then walk past Southwark Cathedral and along the Thames Path.

Address: 21 New Globe Walk, Bankside, London SE1 9DT

Phone/email: Box office: 020 7401 9919; exhibit center: 020 7902 1500/info@shakespearesglobe.org

Hours: Performances begin at 2:00 p.m. and 6:30 or 7:30 p.m. during the week and at 4:00 p.m. on Sunday. The play season runs from late April through early October. The box office is open daily from 10:00 a.m. to 6:00 p.m. and open before all plays.

Exhibition open 9:00 a.m. to 5:30 p.m. daily. Globe Theatre tours available Monday from 9:30 a.m. to 5:00 p.m. and Tuesday through Saturday 9:30 a.m. to 12:30 p.m. Sunday tours 9:30 a.m. to 11:30 a.m. Sam Wana-maker Playhouse tours 1:00 p.m. to 5:00 p.m. on select days. Closed December 24–25.

Time needed: Performance times vary. A tour takes about an hour.

Admission: Exhibition and tour tickets are reasonably priced. There are discounts for children, families, and seniors. Costs for performances vary by location, from the low-budget space for groundlings (standees in front of the stage) to the more noble gallery seats.

Facilities: Restaurant, cafés on-site (no outside food). Toilets and baby-changing areas. Some areas of the theater are not wheelchair accessible.

Website: www.shakespearesglobe.org

Unicorn Theatre

Whereas many theaters offer some programs and performances for children, the Unicorn is a bit more focused—it is a theater built and operated specifically for kids. The current location opened in 2005 in Southwark, not far from Tower Bridge. The Unicorn offers theater-related activities and a changing lineup of performances, helpfully graded by "size": XS for children from birth to age four; S for kids from four to seven; M for kids age seven through twelve; L for children thirteen and over; and the occasional XL for adults.

WHERE? WHEN? £?

UNICORN THEATRE

Location: South Bank, near London's city hall

Address: 147 Tooley Street, Southwark, London SE1 2HZ

Tube: London Bridge station (Northern or Jubilee Line)

Phone: 020 7645 0560

Hours: Performance times vary, but late morning and afternoon times are common.

Time needed: Depends on length of performance/ activity

Admission: Tickets are moderately priced. There are discounts for families. Tickets can be booked online.

Facilities: Snack bar on-site. Toilets and baby-changing areas. Wheelchair accessible.

Website: www.unicorntheatre.com

Start Ramblin'

Where am I going? I don't quite know.
Down to the stream where the king-cups grow—
Up on the hill where the pine-trees blow—
Anywhere, anywhere. I don't know.
—"Spring Morning," by A. A. Milne

Britain is a country of walkers, or "ramblers" in Britspeak. Unlike in some parts of the world, where private property paranoia keeps strangers from walking through the countryside, British walkers have the right to trek through much of the country. There are more than 100,000 miles of public footpaths and rights-of-way in England and Wales—amazing considering the small size of these countries. British hikers refer to themselves as ramblers with good reason, because they truly ramble across the land. Hiking enthusiasts banded together to form a nonprofit Ramblers Association. The group's website (www .ramblers.org.uk) is a good starting point for anyone interested in walking through the British countryside.

The detailed instructions contained in British walking guides can be fun for children to decipher. Arm your kids with trail guides that describe walks using phrases like "go over the stile, turn left at the large oak tree, past the stone wall on your left . . ." Once kids learn that stiles are fence or wall crossings, they are ready for an adventure on the trail.

Wherever you ramble in Britain, pick up information on local walking trails. There is no better way to see the country and get beyond the normal tourist routes. For example, while touring the Cotswolds, we were dismayed when we arrived at Bourton-on-the-Water. The tour books had described a pretty, rural town. The reality of Bourton-on-the-Water on a midsummer day was dozens of tour buses and hordes of visitors. Luckily we were carrying a book detailing off-the-beaten-path walks throughout the country. Using that guide, we went over stiles, through fields, and around cows to tiny Wyck Rissington—a village two miles and centuries removed from Bourton. Wyck Rissington is the quietest village imaginable, with few tourists and no souvenir shops. We ate a Father's Day picnic in an ancient churchyard, then spent a few minutes visiting the village church. A two-mile hike had taken us from the tourist version of the Cotswolds to the real thing.

But hiking is not limited to rural Britain. The Thames Path winds 180 miles from the river's source in rural Gloucestershire to the Thames Barrier below Greenwich. In the process, the path runs through Windsor, Hampton Court, and downtown London.

Strictly speaking, there aren't many hiking trails in town, but London is very much a city for walkers. The Mall—one of the widest and most historic boulevards in London—is closed to vehicles on Sundays so that pedestrians can stroll unimpeded. Before walking here, make sure kids know that the Mall in London isn't home to hundreds of stores and a food court. The Mall is the wide street leading from Buckingham Palace along St. James's Park toward Whitehall and the Admiralty Arch. This is one of the most famous parade routes in London, and you can make your own parade on any Sunday. Properly pronounced, *Mall* rhymes with the word *shall*. And to add to the confusion, there are two parallel streets here: the Mall and Pall Mall, which is a busy street just a few hundred feet north. Pedestrians can safely stroll down the Mall on Sunday; if you try this on Pall Mall, you'll get run over.

Walking in London does present some hazards, primarily when crossing streets. Tourists from most other countries generally look left for oncoming traffic, but because Britons drive on the left, an unwitting tourist may never see the lorry (truck) coming from the right. Smack! One less repeat visitor. Seriously, the only good defensive strategy is to swivel your head when crossing a street in London. Look right, look left, then look right and left again. That way your instincts won't get you killed. Recognizing the potential hazard, London traffic officials have painted the words "look right" or "look left" on the pavement at some pedestrian crossings.

London crosswalks come in three varieties: painted zebra stripes on the pavement, where all traffic should stop for pedestrians; crossings where walkers must wait for a signal to cross; and mere suggestions of crosswalks, where cars aren't required to stop. Zebra-stripe crossings are usually further marked by curbside light poles with round, blinking globes to remind drivers to stop for pedestrians.

Assuming you survive crossing the streets, you can take a walk that traces the outlines of the old wall that surrounded Londinium, the Roman precursor to London. This is a one-and-a-half mile walk between the Museum of London and the Tower of London, with historical markers and glimpses of the old wall along the way.

No, that's not John, Paul, George, or Ringo

For those who want to combine walking with a guided tour, several companies offer walking tours. London Walks is the best-known walking-tour company, but there are several others. Walks usually focus on an area of the city or a historical theme, led by guides who are both personable and knowledgeable. Evening walks featuring Jack the Ripper, ghosts, or pub crawls may not be appropriate for children. We have found only one downside to signing up for a guided walk; by the time the tour starts, you may already have walked so much on your own that you will be too tired to go.

WHERE? WHEN? £?

WALKING TOURS (LONDON WALKS)

Location: Walks start outside Tube stations nearest to the beginning of the walk route.

Address: P.O. Box 1708, London NW6 4LW

Phone/email: 020 7624 3978; recorded information: 020 7624 9255/London@walks.com

Hours: Starting times from about 10:00 a.m. until midafternoon. Evening walks begin at 7:00 or 7:30 p.m.

Time needed: About two hours

Admission: Walks are reasonably priced, and there are discounts for seniors and students. Children under age fifteen walk for free. Multiple-walk discount cards are available. London Walks also offers day trips outside of London.

Website: www.walks.com

Marching around St. James's Park

Fancy a stroll through central London? This three- or four-mile walk takes ninety minutes to four hours, depending on route choices, number of stops, and your pace.

Marching around St. James's Park

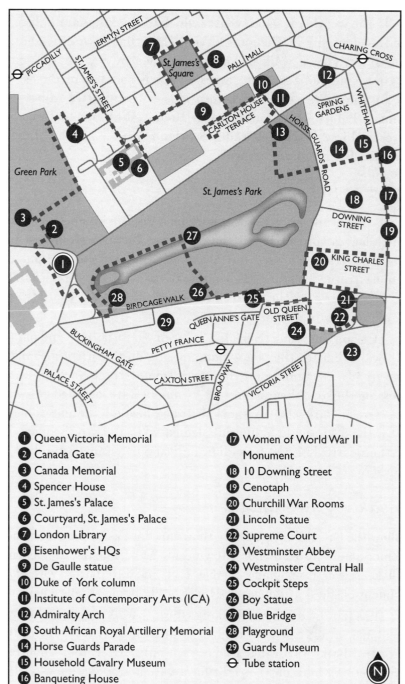

1 Queen Victoria Memorial
2 Canada Gate
3 Canada Memorial
4 Spencer House
5 St. James's Palace
6 Courtyard, St. James's Palace
7 London Library
8 Eisenhower's HQs
9 De Gaulle statue
10 Duke of York column
11 Institute of Contemporary Arts (ICA)
12 Admiralty Arch
13 South African Royal Artillery Memorial
14 Horse Guards Parade
15 Household Cavalry Museum
16 Banqueting House
17 Women of World War II Monument
18 10 Downing Street
19 Cenotaph
20 Churchill War Rooms
21 Lincoln Statue
22 Supreme Court
23 Westminster Abbey
24 Westminster Central Hall
25 Cockpit Steps
26 Boy Statue
27 Blue Bridge
28 Playground
29 Guards Museum
⊖ Tube station

If the weather is good, visitors flock to Buckingham Palace to see the changing of the guard. And while that's a quintessential tourist activity, a walk in and around nearby St. James's Park is a relaxing contrast. St. James's Park is conveniently close to an amazing array of historic locations—Westminster Abbey, St. James's Palace, the Churchill War Rooms, Number 10 Downing Street, Horse Guards Parade, Scotland Yard . . . and did we mention Buckingham Palace?

Start at the Palace

Start this walk by turning your back to Buckingham Palace, which leaves you staring at the ❶ Queen Victoria Memorial and the huge, traffic-clogged but beautiful circle outside the palace. Vehicle traffic has been relegated to two-thirds of the circle; the area closest to the palace is reserved for milling tourists and marching palace guards.

After paying your respects to Queen Victoria, face the palace and walk right to the pedestrian crossing on Constitution Hill, a busy roadway running on the north side of the palace grounds. Crossing the road, bear right to ❷ Canada Gate, a gilded gateway into Green Park. Just a short distance beyond the gate on the left is the ❸ Canada Memorial, dedicated in 1994 to the memory of the nearly 114,000 Canadian military personnel who died in World Wars I and II.

Sneaking through the Alley

Follow the Green Park pathway that runs due east from the Canada Memorial until it dead-ends into Queen's Walk. The tall iron fencing will keep you from going farther east and interfering with government business at Lancaster House or St. James's Palace beyond.

Turn left, heading north along Queen's Walk, peering through the fence at ❹ Spencer House, a historic private palace and ancestral home to Princess Diana's family. After about 800 feet (250 meters), look on the right for a gate and a passageway that actually goes through and under a building. This shortcut is open daily from 6:00 a.m. to 10:00 p.m., and it brings you out onto tiny St. James's Place opposite the Stafford Hotel. Turn right and walk about 200 feet (60 meters) to Spencer House, which is open for guided tours but does not allow children under age ten. Bear left and continue down St. James's Place a short distance to busy St. James's Street.

Yes, street names do get confusing hereabouts. In addition to St. James's Place and St. James's Street, there's also a Little St. James's Street and St. James's Square.

Continue south on St. James's Street, passing Little St. James's Street; after about 500 feet (150 meters), you will arrive at ❺ St. James's Palace. Oddly, although no king or queen has lived here for more than 200 years, St. James's Palace remains the official residence of the sovereign. Various members of the royal family have apartments and offices here, but visitors are not allowed except by special arrangement. The red brick Tudor facade of St. James's certainly looks the part of a royal palace; this is another location where kids can get a close-up look at palace guards in bright red uniforms.

Pell Mell down Pall Mall

Because the guards won't let you into St. James's Palace, turn left onto Pall Mall (street). Just ahead on the right is Marlborough Road, which goes past the ❻ courtyard of St. James's Palace. If you are in the area about ten minutes after the changing of the guard at Buckingham Palace, you can detour a short distance down Marlborough Road to see the guards "retire" in the courtyard of St. James's Palace.

Return to Pall Mall from Marlborough Road and turn right. After about 500 feet (150 meters), turn left into the southwest corner of St. James's Square. The leafy Georgian square was once the most fashionable residential address in this part of London, although today it is more of a home to corporations and upscale clubs.

Strolling clockwise around the square, you'll come to number 14, which houses the **7** London Library. The library's membership has included Agatha Christie, Charles Darwin, Winston Churchill, and Charles Dickens. Tours are by appointment only (and probably not of interest to many children), but you can peek inside to get a feel for this private library.

Number 31 St. James's Square was the **8** headquarters of US general Dwight Eisenhower; plans for the D-Day invasion were formulated here. An equestrian statue of King William III stands at the center of the parklike square—a pleasant place to sit on a nice day, but without a playground or other family attractions.

The Grand Old Duke of York

Exit on the southeast corner of St. James's Square and return to Pall Mall, 100 feet (30 meters) south. Cross Pall Mall, turn right, and then almost immediately turn left down narrow Carlton Gardens. In about 300 feet (90 meters), the road comes to a "T" intersection. Detour right and find the **9** statue of French hero Charles De Gaulle, who had his headquarters here after the German invasion of France in 1940.

Look around the small and beautiful Carlton Gardens, and then head back east on Carlton House Terrace toward the **10** Duke of York column ahead. This 123-foot-tall monument honors the very same Duke of York who, in the children's nursery rhyme, took his ten thousand men and marched them up to the top of the hill and marched them down again. Anyone who has been in the military feels their pain.

March on down the steps next to the duke's column in the direction of the Mall (street) and St. James's Park, just 200 feet (60 meters) away. On your left is the **11** Institute of Contemporary Arts, which describes its collections as avant-garde. Whether this matches your artistic tastes or not, the ICA's café-bar can probably match your taste for a quick and convenient snack and drink.

Into the Park and Looking for Horses

Cross the Mall using the pedestrian crossing just to your right. As you walk, look left and spot the **12** Admiralty Arch; glance right and you'll see Buckingham Palace in the distance. The Mall is a popular parade route in London, and if you've arrived around the time of a celebration, the Mall will be decked out with flags.

Walk down the path ahead, which starts just to the right of the **13** South African Royal Artillery Memorial. Keep straight where the pathway splits, and in about 400 feet (120 meters), turn left. Straight ahead is the expanse of **14** Horse Guards Parade, where you can see the changing of the mounted guards. Be careful crossing Horse Guards Road. There aren't many pedestrian crossings here, but the road can be busy. If you are not arriving in time for the changing of the guards ceremony, never fear, because you can see two horses and guards stationed along Whitehall Road. Just walk across the parade grounds and through the archways in the Horse Guards building ahead. Want even more time with the horses and guards? The **15** Household Cavalry Museum is right here.

10 Downing Street

Turn right, heading south on Whitehall Road. Just across the street is the **16** Banqueting House, all that remains of Whitehall Palace. This is where ill-fated King Charles I met his demise. He stepped out of an upper window onto a platform and was publicly beheaded outside the hall. A tour of this ornate hall doesn't take long.

Continue south on Whitehall a short distance and notice the memorial in the middle of the roadway. This is the **17** National Women of World War II Monument, in memory of the work and sacrifices of Britain's women during the war. This area is the center of much British bureaucratic activity, and "Whitehall" is often synonymous with "government."

In keeping with the governmental theme, the next stop on our walk is ⓲ Downing Street. In all honesty, this isn't much of a stop anymore, since the public isn't allowed to walk on the famous street, much less stroll down to Number 10, where the prime minister lives. So peer through the barricades, but don't expect to see much more than a police officer or two.

Just past Downing Street, again in the middle of Whitehall, is the somber ⓳ Cenotaph, a monument to British soldiers who died in World War I. *Cenotaph* is from the Greek for "empty tomb."

Winston's Bunker

About 200 feet (60 meters) south of the Cenotaph, turn right onto King Charles Street, go through the archways, and continue until the street dead-ends into King Charles Steps. You're walking between the Treasury on the left and the Foreign and Commonwealth Office on the right. But at the stairs, you step back into mid-twentieth-century history. This is where Winston Churchill had his underground command post during much of World War II. The ⓴ Churchill War Rooms are on your left as you descend King Charles Steps. Walk a few feet beyond the entrance, and you're back on Horse Guards Road.

Turn left, heading south on Horse Guards Road. Notice the low concrete wall added to the outside of the ground floor of the building on your left. This is part of the reinforcements added to the treasury building to protect Churchill's war rooms in the subbasement below. Walk about 300 feet (90 meters) on Horse Guards Road and turn left onto Great George Street. Big Ben will come into view ahead, and in about 500 feet (150 meters), the road meets Parliament Square on the right.

Wave to Abe

Turn right into Parliament Square and look closely for the ㉑ statue of US president Abraham Lincoln just ahead on the right—he's easy to overlook when you've got Big Ben and Parliament to your left and Westminster Abbey straight ahead. As a man of law, Lincoln might be pleased to know that his statue is close to Britain's **22** Supreme Court, at the southwest corner of Parliament Square, across the street from Westminster Abbey. The court is open to visitors and a visit to **23** Westminster Abbey is possible at this point.

But this walk continues without going across to the abbey. At the southwest corner of Parliament Square, turn right onto Broad Sanctuary. In 200 feet, you will see a triangular-shaped plaza on your right, in front of the Queen Elizabeth II Conference Centre. Walk across the plaza next to the conference center building. The large white building directly ahead is **24** Westminster Central Hall, operated by the Methodist Church. The café in the lower ground floor of the hall is a convenient spot to get refreshments.

The Old Queen

Turn right onto Storey's Gate and walk north for 250 feet (75 meters), then turn left. This was once a Tudor passageway called Maiden Lane, but when the roadway was widened, it was renamed Old Queen Street—someone had a sense of humor! Property values are astronomical in this area. Walk about 500 feet (150 meters) down Old Queen Street, admiring real estate that is out of reach for most of us. Just as the street turns a little to the left, bear right and look for a literal hole in the wall labeled **25** Cockpit Steps. Walk through the gateway between two buildings. No, you are not trespassing; this is a public passageway that just looks as if it's leading you into someone's backyard.

A few steps ahead you arrive at another quaintly named road: Birdcage Walk. At one time the Royal Menagerie and Aviary was nearby. There is a pedestrian crossing here, so cross over to the other side of Birdcage Walk and turn left.

Into the Park

At the next traffic signal on Birdcage Walk—a pedestrian crossing at Queen Anne's Gate—turn right into St. James's Park. Go past the small white **26** Boy Statue, toward the **27** Blue Bridge over St. James's Park Lake. Stop on the bridge for wonderful views of Whitehall and the London Eye to the right and Buckingham Palace to the left.

At the north end of the bridge, go left and walk along the edge of the lake in the direction of the palace. Keep left at the end of the lake, and you'll reach the park's only **28** playground, which also has toilets and a snack bar. It's not a large playground, but the setting is nice. Make a brief stop here if your children still have energy to play.

Back to the Palace

Exiting the playground, turn right and retrace your steps just 100 feet (30 meters) in the direction of the palace. Turn left and walk a few feet back to Birdcage Walk. Directly across the street is the **29** Guards Museum, where you can learn more about the foot soldiers who guard royal palaces. The shop in the museum is one of the best places in London to buy toy soldiers. To reach the museum, cross over Birdcage Walk and walk left.

If you are not visiting the museum, continue west along Birdcage Walk a very short distance and turn right at Spur Road. Queen Victoria atop her monument appears just ahead, beckoning you to the end of your walk at Buckingham Palace.

Strolling the South Bank

Another pleasant walk covers the South Bank. This almost four-mile (six-kilometer) stroll takes between ninety minutes and four hours, depending on route choices, number of stops, and your pace.

Strolling South Bank

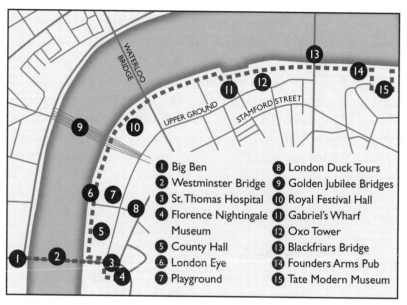

1. Big Ben
2. Westminster Bridge
3. St. Thomas Hospital
4. Florence Nightingale Museum
5. County Hall
6. London Eye
7. Playground
8. London Duck Tours
9. Golden Jubilee Bridges
10. Royal Festival Hall
11. Gabriel's Wharf
12. Oxo Tower
13. Blackfriars Bridge
14. Founders Arms Pub
15. Tate Modern Museum

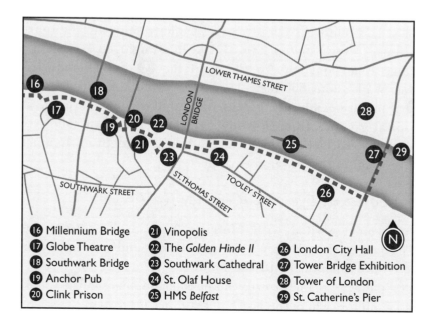

16. Millennium Bridge
17. Globe Theatre
18. Southwark Bridge
19. Anchor Pub
20. Clink Prison
21. Vinopolis
22. The *Golden Hinde II*
23. Southwark Cathedral
24. St. Olaf House
25. HMS *Belfast*
26. London City Hall
27. Tower Bridge Exhibition
28. Tower of London
29. St. Catherine's Pier

On the south bank of the Thames, a portion of the 184-mile-long Thames Path runs right through central London. It is possible to walk much farther in either direction. But let's look at the section on the south bank from Westminster Bridge downstream to Tower Bridge.

Attractions abound along the river in South Bank, and the area offers spectacular views across the water toward the historic monuments of central London, including Parliament, Whitehall, St. Paul's Cathedral, and the Tower of London. The Westminster-to-Tower Bridge route is a great walk to take in conjunction with visits to the Florence Nightingale Museum, the London Eye, the Tate Modern, the Millennium Bridge, the Globe Theatre, the *Golden Hinde II*, the HMS *Belfast*, and the Tower Bridge Exhibition.

Westminster Bridge

The walk starts on Westminster Bridge, where thousands of tourists gawk at and photograph ❶ Big Ben and Parliament. After appreciating the view, turn your back on Big Ben and make your way to the east end of the ❷ bridge.

At this point it's tempting to turn left, following the tourist streams, to the London Eye. But keep straight on Westminster Bridge Road and look to the right for ❸ St. Thomas Hospital. Walk about 800 feet (240 meters), and you will reach the ❹ Florence Nightingale Museum. You can cut through the hospital grounds from Westminster Bridge Road or follow the museum signs farther along the road, bearing right on Lambeth Place Road to the museum entrance.

The London Eye and County Hall

After you've visited with Florence Nightingale, retrace your steps back to the end of Westminster Bridge and turn right along the river embankment to the London Eye, about 900 feet (275 meters) downstream. Crowds can be thick outside the ❺ County Hall complex, where the Eye's ticket office is located.

Keep heading along the pathway past the ❻ London Eye—or stop and go for a ride before continuing your walk. On your right is a ❼ playground and the open space of Jubilee Gardens. Children age eleven and under are welcome to stop, climb, and play at this expansive playground. The surrounding lawns are a popular picnic spot for families. Note that you're within a few hundred feet from where the ❽ London Duck (DUKW) boat tours depart on Chicheley Street.

Golden Jubilee Bridges

About 700 feet (210 meters) beyond the Eye is the once-drab Hungerford railway bridge. Two modern ❾ pedestrian bridges, built in honor of Queen Elizabeth II's Golden Jubilee in 2002, now flank the railway bridge. This walk takes you under Hungerford Bridge; if you want to take a river view photo of the London Eye, detour up onto the first pedestrian bridge and walk about halfway across the river.

The performing spaces of ❿ Royal Festival Hall are to the right as you emerge from under the bridge. This is part of Southbank Centre, built on the site of the 1951 Festival of Britain. The festival celebrated Britain's then-struggling recovery from the economic and physical destruction wrought by World War II.

As you continue along the riverside, enjoy the wonderful views of St. Paul's Cathedral across the Thames. Notice the lampposts along this stretch of the walk. Wrapped around the base are supposedly dolphins, but if that's true, these are the scaliest dolphins imaginable.

Gabriel's Wharf

Especially in good weather, there are food trucks, pop-up restaurants, and bookstalls set up along this route. About one-third of a mile (0.5 kilometer) beyond the Royal Festival Hall is ⓫ Gabriel's Wharf, a festival marketplace with an array of shops, bars, and restaurants. Hungry families can seek out the local gourmet pizza place here or grab some takeout food to eat outside and enjoy great views across the river. Some of the shops in Gabriel's Wharf sell locally designed and produced goods.

Oxo Tower

About 500 feet (150 meters) past Gabriel's Wharf is the distinctive **12** Oxo Tower. At one time, the south bank of the Thames was lined with power-generating stations. You'll see them in London upstream at Battersea and farther downstream at the Tate Modern. In its original incarnation, the Oxo Tower complex was one of these riverside power plants. But the site was rebuilt during the late 1920s, with the art deco tower. The letters O-X-O? Sneaky advertising for the Oxo brand of beef stock cubes that were made here. The letters are windows placed to spell out the brand name after local government authorities denied the company's request to erect huge illuminated signs.

The Oxo Tower complex was redeveloped in the 1990s as residential and commercial space. The tower houses an upscale restaurant, bistro, and bar boasting some of the best views in London, with outdoor seating overlooking the Thames.

Tate Modern

The riverside walk continues past quaintly named Marigold Alley in front of the Oxo Tower. After 800 feet (240 meters), the pathway goes under **13** Blackfriars Bridge. The term Blackfriars dates to the 1300s and comes from the French *frères* (brothers)— monks who wore distinctive black cloaks at the priory nearby on the north bank of the Thames.

The modernized Blackfriars bridges boast solar panels that generate up to half the energy required to operate the Blackfriars rail station on the north bank of the Thames. Continue under the bridges and in about 350 feet (100 meters), you will see the **14** Founders Arms pub on the left, jutting out a bit into the river and with top-notch views.

The next landmark is the **15** Tate Modern. The looming Tate, like the Oxo Tower, started its life as a power plant. Harry Potter fans will recognize the bridge in front of the Tate Modern; the **16** Millennium Bridge was destroyed in the film version of *Harry Potter and the Half-Blood Prince*. And although that event never happened in real life, the bridge did experience some rough times soon after it opened in 2000. The modern pedestrian bridge swayed alarmingly in the wind, earning it the nickname the Wobbly Bridge and causing engineers to scramble to reinforce the structure. The bridge has stood firmly since.

Globe Theatre

You can briefly detour onto the bridge, but then continue downstream just a short distance on the Thames Path to the next star of South Bank—the **17** Globe Theatre. The Globe is a reconstruction opened in 1997, but the foundations of the original Globe lie buried under newer buildings a short distance southeast. Unfortunately, there's nothing to see at the actual site, and Shakespeare fans bearing shovels will be turned away, so continue past the reconstructed Globe and under **18** Southwark Bridge about 500 feet (150 meters) beyond.

In 1564 London experienced a winter so cold that the Thames froze over. Taking advantage of the situation, local residents held a Frost Fair on the ice. Murals under Southwark Bridge depict this frigid event. Just beyond the bridge on the right is the historic **19** Anchor Bankside Pub, which dates from the 1600s. Sitting at the Anchor in 1666, Samuel Pepys recorded his impressions of the Great Fire of London.

Southwark Cathedral

Continue on the Thames Path (also called Bankside), bearing right onto Bank End and then left onto Clink Street and under a railroad bridge. Most families will want to avoid the **20** Clink Prison Museum, which is quite gruesome. Wine tasting is available at the **21** Vinopolis complex just a short stagger down Stoney Street on the right. At the end of Clink Street, you come to the more family friendly **22** *Golden Hinde II*, a replica of Sir Francis Drake's around-the-world ship.

The bowsprit of the *Golden Hinde II* points down winding, narrow Cathedral Street toward nearby **23** Southwark Cathedral. Although the cathedral is not London's most impressive church, it is the oldest Gothic church in the city. Parts of the current building date back to 1220.

Continue to the left on the Thames Path, which is also Montague Close, away from the cathedral; after about 500 feet, go under London Bridge. At this point, you have a choice. You can stop on Montague Street and sing an obligatory rendition of "London Bridge Is Falling Down," attracting scornful glances from local residents and businesspeople. Alternatively, you can simply hum the tune and walk through the tunnel under the bridge, emerging onto Tooley Street. The London Bridge Experience, located under the bridge, is another scare-them-until-they-scream commercial attraction. Probably too scary for younger kids.

HMS Belfast

Walk about 250 feet (75 meters) along Tooley Street and follow signs pointing left to Thames Path East. There's also a silver Jubilee Walkway marker on the sidewalk (if you pass **24** St. Olaf House, you've gone too far). The river is right ahead at Queen's Walk sign. About a quarter mile (400 meters) downstream is one of the largest ships you will see in your visit to London—the **25** HMS *Belfast*.

It's hard not to notice the jarring contrast between the gray twentieth-century battle cruiser, the ancient Tower of London just across the water, and the modern twenty-first-century buildings just ahead on the Thames Path. For better or worse, modern buildings have sprouted like mushrooms across central London, and many of them are visible along this walk. They've taken on peculiar names like the Gerkin, Cheesegrater, Shard, and Darth Vader's helmet. No doubt your kids can come up with their own names for these modern edifices. One such new structure is the headquarters of the Greater London Authority, about 800 feet (240 meters) downstream from the HMS Belfast. This is ㉖ London's city hall.

For one of the best views of London, head for the top of the Shard. This modern pyramid is near Southwark Cathedral. The View from the Shard gives visitors a 360-degree panorama on its two main observation decks—one enclosed at level 69, and one partially open to the skies on level 72.

Tower Bridge

The South Bank walk ends 500 feet ahead at ㉗ Tower Bridge, one of the most iconic spots in a city filled with icons. If your family still has a bit of energy, walk partway across the bridge and tour the Tower Bridge Exhibition or continue on to the ㉘ Tower of London. Those who have walked enough can relax on a return to Westminster Bridge via the riverboat service from nearby ㉙ St. Catherine's Pier.

Find the Wild Kingdom

It was a very sunny Saturday and the zoo was crowded with families. The Dursleys bought Dudley and Piers large chocolate ice creams at the entrance and then, because the smiling lady in the van had asked Harry what he wanted before they could hurry him away, they bought him a cheap lemon ice pop. It wasn't bad, either, Harry thought, licking it as they watched a gorilla scratching its head who looked remarkably like Dudley, except that it wasn't blond.

—*Harry Potter and the Philosopher's Stone*, by J. K. Rowling

---

London Zoo

London is not a prime travel destination for wildlife seekers. There are pigeons in Trafalgar Square, exotic waterfowl in St. James's Park, and even reports of urban-adapted foxes wandering parts of the city. But most London animals tend to be of the captive variety, and the best spot for observing animal wildlife in London is the zoo in Regent's Park. The London Zoo may not meet all the criteria for a must-see tourist attraction, especially for those who have visited zoos in other cities. But for families traveling with children, the London Zoo may be on the itinerary.

In 1914, at the start of World War I, a Canadian army officer gave an American black bear named Winnie to the zoo. Two zoo visitors, writer A. A. Milne and his son Christopher, transformed the bear into a children's literary classic. Winnie and many other famous zoo residents are history now, and the London Zoo has reinvented itself with a modern theme of "conservation in action." Even with this lofty mission, the zoo knows that visitors want to see cute, playful animals. When sloth bears were reintroduced to the outdoor exhibits, the bears became the zoo's poster children. The zoo's reptile house had a small part in *Harry Potter and the Sorcerer's Stone*.

Operating since 1828, the Regent's Park site is one of the oldest zoos in the world. Zoo highlights include a gigantic aviary where birds fly "free," a Rainforest World exhibit where tropical animals bask (and Londoners swelter) in a constant 80° F humid heat, and a beach and pool for the zoo's penguin colony. The zoo's old aquarium exhibit can be disappointing for anyone who has visited London's modern aquarium at County Hall, but keep in mind that London Zoo's venue was the world's first public aquarium.

"I want to show you llama poop," said the four-year-old to his father. The Animal Adventure children's zoo and playground is a highlight of the London Zoo, not because it includes many exotic species, but because children can get close-up views and interact with the animals here. Kids can observe animals living in the Treetop Zone and the Roots Zone. Venture to the Splash Zone for some watery play and to the Touch Zone to pet and feed pigs, sheep, goats, and donkeys.

For visitors who live in places without a zoo nearby, the London Zoo may be a worthwhile stop, even with the relatively high price of admission. Tourists who live near a city with a more modern or less expensive zoo may want to bypass the London Zoo.

Face-to-face at Animal Adventure

The London Zoo covers thirty-six acres in the northern corner of Regent's Park and is bisected by Regent's Canal. An interesting way to get to and from the zoo is to take a boat along Regent's Canal (see the "Go Cruisin'" section).

WHERE? WHEN? £?

LONDON ZOO

Location: On the northern edge of Regent's Park

Tube: Camden Town station (Northern Line). Requires a fifteen-minute walk; this station is exit-only at peak weekend periods. An alternative is Regent's Park station (Bakerloo Line) and a slightly longer walk through the park.

Address: Outer Circle, Regent's Park, London NW1 4RY

Phone: 020 7722 3333

Hours: Open daily from 10:00 a.m. to 6:00 p.m. in the peak season (July through early September). During the rest of the year, the zoo closes between 4:00 and 5:30 p.m., based on daylight hours. Last admission is one hour before closing. Closed December 25.

Time needed: Two hours or so (depends on how much you like zoos)

Admission: Tickets are expensive, but there are discounts for children and seniors. Kids under age three get in free. Online booking avoids ticket lines and provides a slight discount. Family tickets are available only online. Priority/fast track tickets available, but cost even more.

Facilities: Cafés, snack bars on-site. Outdoor picnic sites. Toilets and baby-changing areas. Some areas of the zoo are not wheelchair accessible.

Website: www.londonzoo.co.uk

Something Fishy on the Thames

London boasts a modern aquarium on the south bank of the Thames within walking distance of Big Ben. The Old County Hall, formerly a quasi city hall for London-area governments, has been converted into hotels, shops, the London Dungeon, and the world-class London Aquarium.

With its multimillion-liter tanks, the Sea Life London Aquarium is one of Britain's largest, and it rivals US aquariums in Boston, Baltimore, or Long Beach. Most children will enjoy the sharks in the Pacific Ocean tank, the piranhas in the tropical exhibit, and the rain forest experience. The aquarium is home to thousands of sea critters, including some that kids can touch. A coral reef exhibit combines the usual aquatic specimens with interactive audiovisual presentations.

County Hall houses an upscale Marriott Hotel and a moderately priced Premier Inn that is popular with touring family groups. The location is convenient for central London. Visitors who stay here are within walking distance of Parliament, Westminster Abbey, and the London Eye.

WHERE? WHEN? £?

LONDON AQUARIUM

Location: On the south bank of the Thames, just across Westminster Bridge from Big Ben and near the London Eye
Tube: Westminster station (Circle or District Line), then walk across Westminster Bridge
Address: County Hall, Westminster Bridge Road, London SE1 7PB
Phone/email: 087 1663 1678 (UK calls only)/ sllondon@merlinentertainments.biz

Hours: Monday through Thursday 10:00 a.m. to 7:00 p.m. Open until 8:00 p.m. during school holidays and closes early on select days (check website). Last admission one hour before closing. Closed December 25.

Time needed: Two hours

Admission: Tickets are moderately expensive, but in line with similar aquariums elsewhere. There are numerous ticket packages and discounts for children, families, and students. Online tickets cost less than those purchased at the ticket office. Combination Aquarium–London Eye tickets are available.

Facilities: No food on-site, but several food options are nearby in the County Hall complex. Toilets and baby-changing areas. Fully wheelchair accessible.

Website: www.visitsealife.com/london

And Something Fowl

Just over three miles west (as the duck flies) from Buckingham Palace, London's wildfowl make themselves at home in one hundred acres of wetlands. The London Wetland Centre opened in 2000 on the site of an abandoned waterworks, creating a wetland habitat that attracts wildlife and human visitors alike.

The center staff has counted some 180 wild bird species at the site. The Wetland Centre is not a top tourist destination, but it is popular with local school groups and nature lovers. The education center and its displays will interest budding naturalists.

WHERE? WHEN? £?

LONDON WETLAND CENTRE

Location: Just west of central London, on the south bank of the Thames, about halfway between Buckingham Palace and Kew Botanic Gardens

Transportation: Hammersmith station (Piccadilly, District, or Hammersmith & City Line) with a short ride on a connecting "duck bus" (bus 283). Also by train from London Waterloo station to Barnes station, with a fifteen-minute walk or connecting bus.

Address: Queen Elizabeth's Walk, Barnes, London SW13 9WT

Phone/email: 020 8409 4400/info.london@wwt.org.uk

Hours: In summer months, open daily from 9:30 a.m. to 6:00 p.m. In winter the center closes at 5:00 p.m. Last admission is one hour before closing. Closes early on December 24, and closed on December 25.

Time needed: One or two hours

Admission: Tickets are reasonably priced. There are discounts for families, children, and seniors.

Facilities: Restaurant on-site. Toilets and baby-changing areas. Wheelchair accessible.

Website: www.wwt.org.uk (select London location)

Watch the Changing of the Guard

They're changing the guard at Buckingham Palace—
Christopher Robin went down with Alice.
We saw a guard in a sentry-box.
"One of the sergeants looks after their socks,"
Says Alice.
They're changing the guard at Buckingham Palace—
Christopher Robin went down with Alice.
They've great big parties inside the grounds.
"I wouldn't be King for a hundred pounds,"
Says Alice.
—"Buckingham Palace," by A. A. Milne

What tourist visits London without witnessing the changing of the guard? Some do, of course, but we suspect that almost none of them are touring with kids. Thankfully, there are more ways to see changing guards than just crowding against the fence at Buckingham Palace. First, visiting families should know that there are two separate guard ceremonies: the palace guard at Buckingham and the mounted guard down the Mall at Whitehall.

Of the two, the mounted horse guards ceremony is more accessible. The site of the ceremony, a large open plaza called Horse Guards Parade, provides room to spread out and get a good view of the event. The palace of Whitehall once stood in this part of London, and the Horse Guards Parade was the tiltyard of the palace where jousting (tilting) tournaments were held. In a more modern incarnation, the Horse Guards Parade was the site of the beach volleyball competition for the 2012 Olympics.

The guards are mounted troopers of the Household Cavalry, also known as the Sovereign's Life Guard. Hearing this name, children may ask: "If these guys are lifeguards, then where's the swimming pool?" There is no swimming pool, but if your

Horse Guards Parade

kids love horses, this is *the* guard ceremony to see. The mounted horse guards are resplendent with their swords, shining silver breastplate armor, and, of course, beautifully groomed horses. Afterward, your children can pet the two horses standing guard on the Whitehall Street side of Horse Guards Parade. This makes an excellent photo op, but watch where you step!

The horse guards ceremony is a popular event that lasts about thirty minutes. Visitors can also glimpse the horse guards trooping to and from the ceremony. The guards leave the Knightsbridge Barracks in Hyde Park at about 10:30 in the morning and return around noon.

In mid-June, Horse Guards Parade is the site of the ceremonial Trooping the Color—a review of troops to mark the monarch's official birthday. Obtaining tickets to this popular event takes a lot of preplanning and some luck. It's somewhat easier to attend one of the rehearsals held on the weekends preceding the actual event. Massed military bands gather at Horse Guards Parade on two days in June for the Beating Retreat ceremony. This is a chance to see marching bands and hear the tortured sounds of bagpipes in London.

If you are attending the Buckingham Palace guard ceremony, be sure to arrive for the changing of the guard early enough to get a spot up front against the palace fence so children have a good view. Even then, be prepared for pushing and jostling for position by other tourists. If it's too crowded for kids to see, climb up the steps of the nearby Queen Victoria Memorial for a better view. The ceremony is normally performed by the foot guards of the British Army's Household Division. In the summer months, the guards usually wear bright red uniforms with tall bearskin hats (uniforms vary depending on the season). The changing of the palace guard takes place daily at 11:30 a.m. during the summer and on alternate days during the rest of the year.

Before the ceremony, a military band often plays in the palace courtyard. See if your kids can pick out what the band is playing. Their repertoire is not all old military marches; you're likely to hear more current popular music, but nothing too avant-garde (pardon the pun).

Avoid the crush of the Buckingham Palace guard ceremony entirely by walking down the Mall and turning left onto Marlborough Road. After the shift change at Buckingham Palace, a portion of the guard troop marches away and follows this route to St. James's Palace. Here visitors can see another ceremony. This

is not as elaborate as the ceremony at Buckingham Palace, but it is a lot less crowded, onlookers are closer to the action, and there's no fence to block the view.

Heavy metal music at the palace

WHERE? WHEN? £?

CHANGING OF THE MOUNTED HORSE GUARDS

Location: Horse Guards Parade, a plaza just off Horse Guards Road near the east end of St. James's Park

Tube: Westminster station (Circle or District Line), Charing Cross station (Bakerloo or Northern Line), or Embankment station (Bakerloo, Circle, District, or Northern Line).

Hours: The horse guard changes at 11:00 a.m. (10:00 on Sunday). The ceremony may be canceled in wet weather. In addition, two mounted soldiers stand guard along Whitehall (the street) between 10:00 a.m. and 4:00 p.m.

Time needed: Ceremony lasts thirty minutes

WHERE? WHEN? £?

CHANGING OF THE GUARD AT BUCKINGHAM PALACE

Location: Buckingham Palace

Tube: Green Park station (Jubilee, Victoria, or Piccadilly Line), St. James's Park station (Circle or District Line), or Victoria station (Circle, District, or Victoria Line)

Hours: Daily at 11:30 a.m. during the spring and summer, and every other day during the rest of the year.

Time needed: Ceremony lasts forty-five minutes, but arrive early to get a decent spot. (The ceremony may be canceled in wet weather.)

Website: www.royal.gov.uk (search for "royal events and ceremonies"); there is also a Changing the Guard app in the iTunes store.

Go for the Gold — Olympic Park

London is no newcomer to the Olympics. In 1908, the Summer Games were scheduled to be held in Rome, but plans were scuttled by the eruption of nearby Mt. Vesuvius. London stepped up to host what some call the first modern Olympics. In the aftermath of World War II, London helped restart the Olympics. Despite devastation and postwar shortages, London managed to stage the 1948 Olympics using Wembley Stadium for many events and housing athletes at schools and former military camps all over the city.

Much changed in the sixty-four years between the 1948 London Olympics and the 2012 Summer Games, and one of the most dramatic changes to the London landscape was seen in a once-decrepit section of East London. The construction of Olympic Park transformed a wasteland into a modern sports complex. The Queen Elizabeth Olympic Park includes housing, shopping, parks, hotels, and offices—all served by a twenty-first-century public transportation network.

Before the 2012 Olympics, tourists were rare in this part of London. That's not quite strong enough—before the 2012 Olympics, tourists did not come here, period. Why would they?

Calling the London Olympics site a former wasteland is no overstatement. The area was piled high with rubble dumped after World War II bombing attacks on London; there was so much debris that the River Lea, which runs through the area, was almost invisible. The soil was saturated with heavy metals and nasty industrial pollutants.

This was about as far as you could get from the London that tourists want to enjoy.

The debris is long gone, the soil scrubbed clean, and a massive construction project transformed the area into an Olympics showcase. Just under one square mile, Queen Elizabeth Olympic Park is compact. The restoration of the River Lea and the planting of thousands of trees along its banks put the "park" into the park.

The future of Olympic Park is still being written. It was designed to have a life after the Olympic Games. Some of the big venues remain on the site, some have been reconfigured, and some are gone. Professional football (soccer) matches are held in the reconfigured Olympic Stadium. Swimming events continue at the aquatics center—what bigger thrill for the aspiring young swimmers in your family than to plunge into the same pool where Michael Phelps won six medals? The London Aquatics Centre welcomes visitors, and a day pass is reasonably priced.

Cyclists can take to the Olympic trail at the Lee Valley Velopark. The cycling center offers fully equipped mountain biking sessions for competent riders age ten and up and BMX sessions for riders age seven and up. Kids over age twelve can race around the iconic Olympic Velodrome track. The less athletically inclined might opt for a ride to the top of the spiraling ArcelorMittal Orbit. The views from the top are terrific.

Sporting events will continue to draw visitors, and the former Olympics site has been transformed into a rather nice park. The Stratford City megamall is a retail destination. Museums and other cultural venues are planned for the area. But whether the site ever qualifies as a top-tier London tourist destination remains to be seen.

WHERE? WHEN? £?

OLYMPIC PARK

Location: Stratford, East London

Transportation: Stratford International rail station is served by high-speed trains from London's St. Pancras station. Stratford Regional station is a stopping point for the Docklands Light Railway, the Tube (Central or Jubilee Line), and the Overland commuter rail service.

Websites: queenelizabetholympicpark.co.uk (park); uk.westfield.com/stratfordcity (shopping);

www.visitleevalley.org.uk (cycling);

aarcelormittalorbit.com (observation tower)

Go down the River

The Thames will take us to London town,
"Of wonderful beauty and great renown."
The dew goes up and the rain comes down,
To carry us safely to London town.
—"The Thames," by M. M. Hutchinson

Greenwich

Here's a geography quiz for older kids: What is the latitude and longitude of London? Give up? At about fifty-two degrees north latitude, London is roughly in line with Calgary, Canada—a lot farther north than you might expect. The second part of the answer is more significant. London's longitude is nearly zero degrees; the city sits only a few miles west of the prime meridian, the longitudinal line dividing the Earth into Eastern and Western Hemispheres. The suburban London town of Greenwich is home to the prime meridian.

Because time is such an important player here, it is hard to visit Greenwich and not check the time every minute or so. Greenwich Mean Time is a standard used by scientists, navigators, militaries, and travelers throughout the world. Once they grasp the significance of Greenwich Mean Time, school-age kids can determine the time difference to their hometowns.

Taking the boat down the Thames to Greenwich is fun even if your kids don't give a hoot about longitude and Greenwich Mean Time. (See the "Go Cruisin'" section for more information on boat trips.) But even the most uninterested kids will enjoy a visit to the Royal Observatory in Greenwich, and they might learn something, too. Interactive exhibits teach the importance of longitude to seaborne navigation. Early explorers often sailed in circles because they could measure latitude (distance from the equator) using the angle of the sun on the horizon, but they had no way to accurately measure longitude (distance east or west).

The Royal Observatory was founded in 1675 by King Charles II, who appointed John Flamsteed as astronomer royal. Flamsteed's marching orders were specific: find a way to measure longitude at sea. Given the competition among England, France, and Spain for control of the seas, solving the navigation problem was the Apollo moon project of its day. "Mission Control"—Greenwich's observatory building—was designed by Sir Christopher Wren.

A detailed explanation of longitudinal navigation is beyond the scope of this book, but the basic premise is that accurate timekeeping is essential to accurate navigation. Thus, time-keeping became a key function of the observatory. Every day at precisely 1:00 p.m., an orange ball slides down a pole on top of the observatory. In times past, ships on the Thames would set their clocks ("chronometers" to you navigators) by this ball. As with many events in England, there is no reason to continue the tradition, but the time ball continues to drop each day, and tourists enjoy it. Greenwich Mean Time remains a world standard for timekeeping, although technically it has been replaced by Coordinated Universal Time.

Continuing with Longitudinal Navigation 101: another key to navigation is establishing a uniform starting point—the zero or prime meridian line. In 1884, the International Meridian Conference set that line in Greenwich and established the concept of twenty-four worldwide time zones. The prime meridian runs right through the Royal Observatory and is marked on the pavement and walls of the building. A green laser light cuts across the nighttime Greenwich skies highlighting the meridian. The meridian officially divides West from East. At the observatory, this dividing line provides entertainment for visitors, who can stand with one foot in the Western Hemisphere and one foot in the Eastern (or put a foot on the line and balance between east and west).

You can explore Greenwich's association with the sea at other local sites, including the Old Royal Naval College and

On the line in Greenwich

the National Maritime Museum. Kids may enjoy the Maritime Museum, especially the Children's Gallery, where they can explore the spaces of the museum's *Seahorse* ship mock-up and fight pirates through interactive games. The Maritime Museum is a good mixture of high tech and history. There are plenty of pictures of old dead navy guys and fleets of ship models, as well as interesting audiovisual and computer simulations.

The Maritime Museum is also home to the Admiral Nelson exhibit. Or perhaps we should call it the Nelson shrine. The gallery is dominated by Nelson memorabilia, including the bullet-holed dress uniform worn when Nelson met his death at the Battle of Trafalgar. There is plenty of dry historical material here—items that many kids will skip—but some of the computer-animated battle displays will attract young warriors.

While in Greenwich, sailors in the family may be able to tour one of the world's most famous sailing ships. The permanently dry-docked *Cutty Sark* is the last survivor of the clipper ships that sailed around Cape Horn bringing tea from China. The ship survived thousands of nautical miles but nearly perished in a dramatic 2007 fire while undergoing repairs.

The Greenwich Market, just a few steps from the *Cutty Sark*, is a good spot to stop, grab a bite to eat, and browse the stalls. The market features antiques and collectibles on Tuesday, Thursday, and Friday. Crafts and food dominate other days.

Another oddity in Greenwich is the Queen's House. Take a close look at this small palace. It seems awfully familiar, doesn't it? When American visitors learn that this building was once known as the White House, the connection becomes uncanny. The name refers to the building's white plaster facade, but the architecture could have been a model for the White House in Washington. Amazingly, in compact Greenwich, three landmarks have been designated as World Heritage Sites by the United Nations: the Queen's House, the former Royal Naval College, and the Old Royal Observatory (plus surrounding parkland). For more information, see the Visit Greenwich website (www.visitgreenwich.org.uk).

Greenwich is also a stop on the Sir Walter Raleigh trivia tour. A muddy Greenwich street is supposedly where Sir Walter laid his cloak over a puddle to protect the feet of Queen Elizabeth I. The royal family hardly returned the favor; Raleigh was later imprisoned and executed (see "The Tower of London" section).

Greenwich was once a peaceful village on the Thames. Given its association with timekeeping and navigation, a group of influential Britons saw a unique opportunity to focus 2000's millennium celebrations on Greenwich. They developed an ambitious theme park called the Millennium Dome, now known as the O2 Arena. Once featured in a James Bond movie, the structure was planned as a one-year exhibition during 2000, but the venue continues to be used for concerts and events.

The O2 Arena is located along the Thames, just downriver from old Greenwich. At more than 1,000 feet in diameter and 160 feet high, the dome is undeniably huge. Adventure seekers can even clamber across the huge sloping roof at the Up at the O2 climbing venue. See the O2 website for details (www.theo2.co.uk).

Just five miles down the Thames from central London, Greenwich is easy to reach by boat, the Tube, or the Docklands Light Railway. As you might expect, most children vote for the boat trip (and on a nice day, they're right). Here's a rundown of the easiest ways to get to Greenwich:

- Taking the Tube? The Underground's Jubilee Line goes to the Greenwich North station, the closest stop for the O2, but not very close to other Greenwich sites.

- Want to try the Docklands Light Railway? This automated above ground commuter line has a station just steps from the *Cutty Sark* in Greenwich. The Docklands Light Railway connects with the Tube near the Tower of London.

- Thinking about a boat? If you have the time and the weather is good, a boat cruise is a perfect way to see the Thames and get to Greenwich.

- What about a cablecar? That's right, modern cable cars whisk visitors over the Thames near the O2. The views are worth a roundtrip.

For more information on boat trips, read the "Go Cruisin'" section; for more information on the Tube, see "Getting around Town." It is also possible to reach Greenwich by train from several London rail stations. The Greenwich rail station is about a ten-minute walk to the town's tourist attractions. The Maze Hill station is about a five-minute walk to the National Maritime Museum. There are also local buses from Greenwich rail station.

Where? When? £?

National Maritime Museum, Royal Observatory, and Queen's House

Location: Greenwich, near the riverfront

Address: National Maritime Museum, Park Row, Greenwich SE10 9NF; Royal Observatory, Blackheath Avenue, Greenwich SE10 8XJ

Phone/email: General information: 020 8312 6608/ bookings@rmg.co.uk

Hours: Open daily from 10:00 a.m. to 5:00 p.m. Last admission is thirty minutes before closing. Portions of the Maritime Museum are open until 8:00 p.m. on Thursday. Closed December 24–26 and reduced hours on December 31 and January 1.

Time needed: Two to three hours or more for all three sites (museum, observatory, and Queen's House)

Admission: Maritime Museum, Queen's House, and Royal Observatory Astronomy Centre are free, except for special exhibits. Tickets for the rest of the Royal Observatory are moderately priced. Tickets can be booked online.

Facilities: Restaurant, café, and snack bar in museum. Café at observatory. Toilets and baby-changing areas. Most areas of the museum are wheelchair accessible, but parts of the observatory have limited access.

Website: www.rmg.co.uk

WHERE? WHEN? £?

THE *CUTTY SARK*

Location: On the waterfront, near the passenger ferry dock in Greenwich

Address: King William Walk, Greenwich SE10 9HT

Phone/email: 020 8312 6608/ bookings@rmg.co.uk

Hours: Open daily from 10:00 a.m. to 5:00 p.m. Last admission at 4:00 p.m. Closed December 24–26 and reduced hours December 31 and January 1.

Time needed: About one hour

Admission: Tickets are moderately priced. Advance online purchase is recommended.

Facilities: Café on-site. Toilets and baby-changing areas.

Website: www.rmg.co.uk

Thames River Barrier

Visitors to Greenwich can continue down the Thames to visit a modern engineering wonder—the flood barriers that protect London from the ravages of the rising river. If your kids are fascinated by dams, bridges, and other big public works projects, they may enjoy a visit to the Thames River Barrier Information Centre. Once the most futuristic structure on the Thames, the barrier is a minor tourist attraction. However, residents upstream in Greenwich would never take the barrier for granted, because without it, parts of their town would be under water during tidal surges.

This is the world's largest movable flood barrier; when it is raised, its clamshell floodgates are each five stories high. Visitors who arrive on the day of the scheduled monthly systems test don't have to wait for a flood to see the barriers in action. But even when the barriers aren't operating, the visitors' center offers informative exhibits and working models. A park with a play area and restaurant overlooks the barrier on the north side of the river, but there is no direct access between the park and the information center. There are also river sightseeing cruises that sail past the Thames Barrier but do not stop.

Where? When? £?

Thames River Barrier

Location: On the River Thames, downstream from Greenwich

Transportation: There is rail service from Charing Cross and London Bridge rail stations to Woolwich Charlton station or Woolwich Dockyard station (fifteen-minute walk to the barrier). Taxis are available at Woolwich Arsenal rail station. Bus service is also available from east London. The Docklands Light Railway stops at Pontoon Dock for access to the Thames Barrier Park only.

Address: 1 Unity Way, Woolwich, London SE1 5NJ

Phone/Email: 020 8305 4188/ learningcentre@environment-agency.gov.uk

Hours: The information center is open Thursday through Sunday from 10:30 a.m. to 5:00 p.m. Last admission is thirty minutes before closing. Closed December 25–26.

Time needed: One hour

Admission: Tickets are reasonably priced.

Website: www.gov.uk/the-thames-barrier

Go up the River

Some of the world's best gardens are at Kew, just a few miles upstream from central London. A trip up the River Thames also leads to one of Britain's most historic palaces, Henry VIII's Hampton Court.

Kew—The Smell of Flowers

Mistress Mary, quite contrary,
How does your garden grow?
With silver bells, and cockle shells,
And marigolds all in a row.
—Traditional children's rhyme

Parks have gardens, palaces have gardens, churches have gardens . . . visitors are never far from a garden in London, and it is easy to get garden overload during a visit. But if you want to see the mother of all gardens, then add one more stop: the Royal Botanic Gardens, better known as Kew Gardens.

Kew Gardens has a more important mission than simply providing a lovely spot for visitors to enjoy. Plant conservation is the real goal here, and Kew's collection contains living specimens of more than 10 percent of the world's flowering plants. Another important task at Kew Gardens is to preserve seed samples from *all* the plants on Earth.

For the casual visitor, the real attractions at Kew are the acres of landscaped gardens and glasshouses full of unusual plant displays. There is enough variety to keep green-thumbed visitors fascinated for days. The rest of us, especially those with children, will want to devote two or three hours to simply walking the grounds.

Kew's elaborate glasshouses are full of surprises. In the basement of the Palm House is a kid-sized aquarium exhibit. It is not a high-tech aquarium, but the Kew exhibit is just right for a ten-minute visit. The aquarium thoughtfully provides stepstools that children can use to get eye-to-eye with the fish.

The world's oldest potted plant is at Kew, and anyone who has killed a houseplant will be amazed that this plant has survived since 1775. Kew also claims the world's tallest indoor plant, a replacement for the previous record-holding palm, which literally hit the roof in 2001 and had to be cut down. Children may or may not be impressed with all the plants, but they likely will want to climb the spiral staircases up to the elevated walkways that encircle the tops of the glasshouses. If you lose track of your child, look up. Old buildings, and old plants, require constant maintenance. Some of Kew's aging greenhouses (glasshouses) are undergoing renovation until 2018.

Visitors can take a stroll in the treetops via the Rhizotron and Xstrata Treetop Walkway. Designed by the architects of the London Eye, the walkway opened in 2008. It is nearly 60 feet high and spans more than 600 feet, allowing visitors to experience life in the trees of Kew Gardens.

Even on rainy days, kids can play at Kew's indoor exhibits

Kew's Climbers and Creepers exhibit is a plant-themed indoor/ outdoor playground that mixes learning with play. Kids ages three to nine are free to crawl on and through giant "plants" here. Treehouse Towers, Kew's outdoor playground, is just outside and makes a wonderful play option in nice weather for children ages three to eleven.

Although they are nearly eclipsed by the grandeur of the gardens, a small palace and a quaint royal getaway are tucked into Kew Gardens. Built in 1631, Kew Palace is the smallest royal palace in England. It was home to King George III, who spent time here while suffering from his madness. In 1761, he gave Queen Charlotte a nice little wedding present: a rustic cottage on the Kew grounds equipped with a menagerie of kangaroos, buffalo, and other exotic animals. The cottage and surrounding property remained in the royal family until Queen Victoria turned them over to Kew Gardens in 1897. Kew Palace was fully restored over a decade and opened to the public in 2006.

Although there are restaurants on the premises, Kew is a wonderful place to picnic. Its wide-open grounds and fragrant displays are a relaxing contrast to the bustle of urban sites in downtown London.

WHERE? WHEN? £?

ROYAL BOTANIC GARDENS, KEW

Location: A few miles southwest of central London, along the south bank of the Thames, in the town of Richmond

Tube/train: Kew Gardens station (District Line, London Overground). Trains from London Waterloo station also arrive at Kew Gardens or Kew Bridge rail station.

Address: Royal Botanic Gardens, Kew, Richmond, Surrey TW9 3AB
Phone/email: 020 8332 5655/info@kew.org (gardens); 020 3166 6000/kewpalace@hrp.org.uk (palace)
Hours: Gardens open at 9:30 a.m. daily and close at varying times throughout the year. During the summer, last admission is 6:00 p.m. on weekdays and 7:00 p.m. on weekends. Buildings may open later and close earlier. Closed December 24–25. Palace is open from 10:00 a.m. to 5:30 p.m., April through September. Last admission is 5:00 p.m.
Time needed: Garden: two to three hours or more, perhaps much more for garden lovers. Palace: one hour.
Admission: Tickets are moderately priced. There are discounts for students and seniors. Children under age sixteen (palace) or seventeen (gardens) get in free. Tickets can be booked online. Visiting the palace requires a gardens ticket.
Facilities: Restaurants and snack bars on-site. Picnics are allowed in many areas. Toilets and baby-changing areas. Most areas are wheelchair accessible.
Websites: www.kew.org (Kew Gardens); www.hrp.org.uk (Kew Palace)

Kew — The Hiss of Steam

If you have made the trek to Kew and are not exhausted from roaming the gardens, consider visiting some sights nearby. The London Museum of Water and Steam (formerly the Kew Bridge Steam Museum) is across Kew Bridge from the Royal Botanic Gardens. The museum features several working steam pump engines, a small steam railway, and an outdoor Splash Zone play area. Kew's steam engines once pumped the water supply for West London, and, although the waterworks have been modernized, the giant pumping engines are still on display. On weekends, the museum powers up its huge Cornish steam engines in a great display for kids who like the noise and power of big machines.

WHERE? WHEN? £?

LONDON MUSEUM OF WATER AND STEAM

Location: Just across the river from Kew Gardens, about 500 feet from the north side of Kew Bridge, next to the tall Victorian tower

Tube/train: The closest Tube stations are Gunnersbury and Kew Gardens (District Line), but neither is very close. The Kew Bridge rail station is very convenient, and trains run from there to London's Waterloo rail station.

Address: Green Dragon Lane, Brentford, Middlesex TW8 0EN

Phone/email: 020 8568 4757/ museum@waterandsteam.org.uk

Hours: Open daily 11:00 a.m. to 4:00 p.m. Steam engines run on weekends and holidays only.

Time needed: One hour

Admission: Tickets are reasonably priced, and there are discounts for families, students, and seniors. Children under age five get in free.

Facilities: Café, picnic area on-site. Toilets available. Most areas are wheelchair accessible.

Website: www.waterandsteam.org.uk

Kew — The Sound of Music

The Musical Museum falls into a quirky category of tourist venues. It will never appear on a list of top London-area attractions, but if you are in the vicinity and have an appreciation for automatic musical instruments, plan a brief visit. You'll be treated to lots of music, but no musicians. Here the instruments play themselves: organs, music boxes, pianos, violins, and the Clarabella—sort of a one-man band without the man. Once housed in an old church, the tiny Musical Museum has expanded into larger and more modern quarters.

WHERE? WHEN? £?

THE MUSICAL MUSEUM

Location: Across the river from Kew Gardens, just upstream from Kew Bridge

Tube/train: See Museum of Water and Steam, above.

Address: 399 High Street, Brentford, TW8 0DU

Phone: 020 8560 8108/
fred.stone@musicalmuseum.co.uk

Hours: Open Friday through Sunday, and some holidays, from 11:00 a.m. to 5:00 p.m. Last admission is 4:00 p.m.

Time needed: One hour

Admission: Tickets are reasonably priced, and there are discounts for families, students, and seniors. Children under age five get in free.

Facilities: Tearoom on-site. Toilets available.

Website: www.musicalmuseum.co.uk

Hampton Court Palace — Oh, Henry!

Hampton Court is an extreme example of "keeping up with the Joneses." This elaborate palace was built by the uber-ambitious cardinal Thomas Wolsey in the early 1500s. (Vows of poverty apparently did not apply to the church hierarchy at the time.)

King Henry VIII decided that he liked the palace so much that he wanted one just like it, but instead of building his own, Henry borrowed Hampton Court from Wolsey, giving the cardinal very little choice in the matter.

Much of the intrigue of Henry VIII's reign took place at Hampton Court. Some of Henry's wives enjoyed living at the palace (briefly) before adjourning to accommodations in the Tower of London (again, briefly, and in most cases terminally). Henry expanded Cardinal Wolsey's residence, and Henry's successors altered the building even more, but portions of the original brick Tudor palace are still visible today. The building changed significantly in the 1600s under King William III, who planned to turn the site into an English version of Versailles. William employed Christopher Wren, architect of St. Paul's Cathedral, to convert Hampton Court into one of the finest palaces in Britain.

How to convince children to visit yet another palace? Not to worry. In addition to history and architectural splendor, Hampton Court features Henry VIII's original indoor tennis court, a fantastic garden maze, one of the world's largest grapevines, carriage rides on the grounds, and lots of outdoor space to explore.

Although the lasting impression of Henry VIII may be of Henry the Huge, in his earlier years, the king was fairly athletic and a great tennis fan. In 1530, he had a tennis court built at Hampton Court Palace. Royal tennis is only vaguely like the modern version because this indoor game was played off the walls and ledges surrounding the court. Legend has it that Henry played tennis here while Anne Boleyn was being executed at the Tower of London.

The royal tennis court is open to Hampton Court Palace visitors. King Charles II renovated the court in the late 1600s, and what visitors see today has been essentially unchanged since 1700, the obvious exception being the modern lighting. The court is still in use by members of the local tennis club, and you may be lucky enough to see a game in progress. If so, please observe one basic rule of royal tennis etiquette: spectators must keep quiet!

The chimneys of Hampton Court Palace

One of the most popular features of Hampton Court is the maze built on the palace grounds for King William III. Some kids attack the problem of the maze logically, tracking their position by the angle of the sun, or taking only left turns, or using some other semiscientific approach. Others abandon all logic and just run helter-skelter through the maze. We don't know which way works best, but the maze is a challenge for adults and children alike. If you buy a ticket to see the palace interior, admission to the maze is included; otherwise, there is a small fee to get lost here.

Another interesting stop on the palace grounds is the Great Vine of 1769. The vine is one of the world's largest single grapevines, so immense that it has its own greenhouse and root care field. The old vine is still going, producing a large crop of grapes every year. The palace gardens alone are worth the trip to Hampton Court. Admission to the palace's formal gardens is included with overall admission, or you can purchase garden-only tickets. But it costs nothing to visit much of the grounds, so many tourists and local residents simply stroll through or picnic near the palace. A large tearoom is located on the old palace tiltyard; you can enjoy your tea where Tudor knights once jousted.

Although many of Hampton Court's highlights are on the outside, the palace interior is amazing in its own right. Part Versailles, part Tudor brick palace, it is unlike any other palace in Europe. Children are often interested in the cavernous Tudor kitchens, which look as if cooks are in the midst of preparing a feast (or maybe just a snack to satisfy Henry VIII's appetite). Adults gaze slack-jawed at Henry VIII's opulent Chapel Royal and William III's baroque state apartments.

Hampton Court is the site of a mammoth flower show held in July. Visitors who arrive during the show can expect large crowds, but they will be able to tour a phenomenal gardening exhibition. Admission to the show is separate from admission to the palace, and the show tickets are fairly expensive for the casual visitor.

In December and January, a temporary ice-skating rink is set up in front of the palace, livening up the site during an otherwise slow tourism period. There are also special events during the regular season and holiday periods.

WHERE? WHEN? £?

HAMPTON COURT PALACE

Location: East Molesey, Surrey, about ten miles southwest of central London

Transportation: About thirty minutes by train from London's Waterloo station to Hampton Court station, just a short walk from the palace. Riding the Tube to Richmond and a bus to Hampton Court takes a lot longer. If time is no issue, consider a leisurely four-hour boat trip up the Thames from Westminster Pier in London.

Address: Hampton Court, East Molesey, Surrey KT8 9AU

Phone/email: 084 4482 7777 (recorded info, UK calls only); 020 3166 6000 (outside UK)/ hamptoncourt@hrp.org.uk

Hours: From late March through late October, the palace is open daily from 10:00 a.m. to 6:00 p.m. The rest of the year, the palace closes at 4:30 p.m. Last admission is one hour before closing. The gardens have longer hours. The palace is closed December 24–26.

Time needed: Three hours

Admission: Tickets are moderately priced, and there are discounts for children, students, seniors, and families. Children under age five get in free. Garden-only tickets are also available. Tickets may be booked online.

Facilities: Self-service restaurant and cafés. Outdoor picnic spots. Playroom, toilets and baby-changing areas. Some rooms of the palace are not wheelchair accessible.

Website: www.hrp.org.uk

PART THREE

Let's Take a Field Trip!

London Is Great. Why Leave?
Off to Windsor
Off to Oxfordshire
Baby, You Can Drive My Car
Train Wizardry

London Is Great. Why Leave?

London has enough to keep a touring family busy for weeks, so why even consider traveling outside this fascinating city? Well, for overseas visitors, it seems a shame to travel all the way to Britain and not see more of the country than just the capital. The remedy is a field trip—rent a car or take a train and explore some piece of England. This is a compact and eminently accessible land. Although the focus of this book is London (and nearby places such as Greenwich and Hampton Court), we'll give you a taste of what lies farther afield by describing a few gems in the surrounding areas:

- Nearby Windsor with its famous castle
- Oxford's Blenheim Palace
- Stone circles

In addition, we'll provide some survival tips in case you're considering driving in Britain.

Off to Windsor

Although Windsor is within London's suburbs, a family trip here is the perfect opportunity to get away from downtown, see a little of the countryside, and visit a historic town on the Thames. Windsor Castle, the central focus of the town, is one of the most elaborate castles/palaces in the greater London area. Windsor is an easy thirty- to fifty-minute train ride from downtown London, so this first field trip requires no driving.

Field Trip!

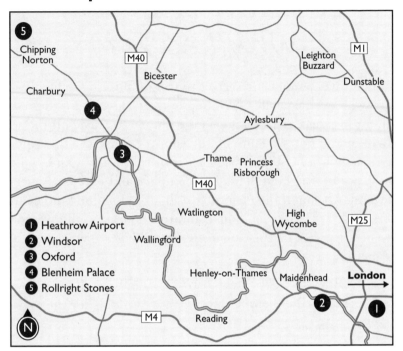

Chipping Norton
M40
Bicester
Leighton Buzzard
M1
Dunstable
Charbury
Aylesbury
Thame
Princess Risborough
M40
Watlington
High Wycombe
M25
1 Heathrow Airport
2 Windsor
3 Oxford
4 Blenheim Palace
5 Rollright Stones
Wallingford
Henley-on-Thames
Maidenhead
London
Reading
M4
N

The Castle

More than 900 years ago, William the Conqueror chose the site for Windsor Castle on a hill above the River Thames. Like the Tower of London, Windsor was part of the Norman king's plans to subdue and maintain control over England. The strategically placed castle was one day's march from London and guarded the city's western flank. Subsequent kings and queens used Windsor as a part-time residence and a refuge from wars, plagues, and uprisings. What has evolved at Windsor is part Norman castle and part royal palace.

Unlike Hampton Court Palace, Windsor Castle is still used by Britain's royal family. Because the castle is a home, a visit here presents children with an opportunity to search for real-life domestic touches. Visitors may observe pet cats, resident children walking to school, or staff members off to play tennis. Just as at

Buckingham Palace, keep an eye on the flagpole. A Union Jack means nothing special, but if the royal standard (the lion flag) appears above the Norman keep at Windsor Castle, the royals have arrived. During one visit, the Union Jack was flying when we entered the castle and began our tour. After our tour, we hit the toilets; when we came out, the royal standard was flying. We missed the arrival of the queen while we were in the loo!

The whole family will probably enjoy a visit to Windsor Castle. Some rooms have extensive displays of armor, which many kids find interesting, but all those staid, ornate royal apartments can get tedious. So a Windsor highlight for many children is Queen Mary's dollhouse. This is one of the largest, most elaborate dollhouses imaginable, truly fit for a queen. The castle also offers family activity trail guides.

During a few weeks each year (usually in August and September) visitors can climb to the top of Windsor's Round Tower. A separate behind-the-scenes tour is also available for the castle's Great Kitchen.

And for kids who have not had their fill of guards changing, Windsor Castle boasts a fairly impressive ceremony. Guard changing takes place at 11:00 a.m. Monday through Saturday,

Windsor walls and the Round Tower

April through July. In other months, the ceremony is held every other day at 11:00 a.m. except Sunday, and the schedule alternates monthly between odd- and even-numbered days.

One of the most impressive buildings in the castle complex is St. George's Chapel, completed in 1475 and a stellar example of medieval architecture. Eighteen kings and queens are buried here, so, yes, Windsor has a full complement of "old dead guys." The chapel is often staffed with enthusiastic, knowledgeable volunteer tour guides. On one visit, a grandfatherly volunteer took extra time to show off the chapel to our kids, pointing out items of interest to children—a welcome personal touch. The chapel is closed to the public on Sunday and frequently for special events.

Touring Windsor Castle today, visitors see no real evidence of the major fire that destroyed parts of the castle in 1992, but the fire is still a relatively fresh memory here. Young visitors might be interested in the story of the fire and the heroic efforts to save priceless art and furnishings from the burning building. About one-fifth of the castle was damaged or destroyed; restoration was completed in 1997 at the cost of almost £36.5 million. Ironically, the loss at Windsor was actually a gain for London tourists, since Buckingham Palace was first opened to visitors in part to help raise money to restore Windsor Castle.

Windsor is a pleasant place to take a walk. The Long Walk is an arrow-straight road that runs from the east side of Windsor Castle to a statue of King George III nearly three miles away. Closed to most traffic, the roadway is lined by the trees and fields of Windsor Home Park. This is an ideal spot to let children burn off excess energy. They can take off running down the Long Walk, but of course you may have to chase them.

Occasionally, visitors to Windsor Home Park can also tour Frogmore House, a royal country estate and the burial place of Queen Victoria and Prince Albert. This was a royal house, not a palace, and it is a contrast to the formal Windsor Castle. The house and gardens are usually open two weekends a year, once in May and again in late August. Group tours are possible at other times.

WHERE? WHEN? £?

WINDSOR CASTLE

Location: The castle looms over the town of Windsor, located on the Thames west of London.

Train: Trains travel from London's Paddington station to the town of Slough, where you change trains for Windsor Central station. The journey takes about thirty-five minutes total, and trains run every twenty minutes during much of the day. There is also train service from London's Waterloo station to Windsor and Eton Riverside station. This avoids a change of trains, but the travel time is about fifty minutes. Both Windsor stations are within walking distance of Windsor Castle.

Address: Windsor, Berkshire SL4 1NJ

Phone/email: 020 7766 7304/ bookinginfo@royalcollection.org.uk

Hours: March through October 9:45 a.m. to 5:15 p.m. In other months, the castle closes at 4:15 p.m. Last admission is seventy-five minutes before closing. Closed December 25–26. Parts of the castle may be closed when the royals are in residence and for special events. St. George's Chapel is closed on Sunday.

Time needed: Two or three hours

Admission: Tickets are moderately priced. There are discounts for children, students, families, and seniors. Children under five get in free. Reduced admission when parts of the castle are closed, and additional tickets are required for the Great Kitchen and when the Round Tower is open. Tickets can be booked online.

Facilities: Family restroom and baby-changing areas. Most areas are wheelchair accessible.

Website: www.royalcollection.org.uk

Windsor — In and around Town

The town of Windsor is an amalgamation of history, peaceful English town life along the Thames, and some tacky intrusions by tourist-oriented businesses. It is disconcerting to see a McDonald's or a Starbucks just outside the massive ancient walls of Windsor Castle. Windsor's many restaurants, souvenir shops, and tourist traps are fairly concentrated, however, and the rest of the town is generally unaffected.

While you're in Windsor, take the pedestrian bridge across the Thames to the tiny town of Eton, which offers some antique shops, a few pubs, and a glimpse of the famous boys' school whose students have included royal princes. Touring Eton College is a bit like visiting Harry Potter's Hogwarts Academy. No magic classes and Quidditch matches here, but the buildings and atmosphere of this ancient school seem vaguely familiar to Harry Potter fans. For information about visits, check the school's website at www .etoncollege.com.

More than anything else, Eton is a quiet town on the river, a contrast to the tourist-thronged Windsor. And the farther you walk into Eton and away from Windsor, the less touristy the town becomes. In Eton, pubs are more likely to be filled with locals, and shops are less likely to hawk cheap souvenirs.

All the King's Swans

Walking over the Windsor-Eton pedestrian bridge, you might catch sight of dozens of swans swimming against the strong current or coasting downstream, always in search of a handout. On one visit, our children counted sixty birds near the bridge.

Since the twelfth century, all the swans on the Thames have been owned by the royal family or by two other groups: the Vintners and the Dyers. In a land of quaint tradition, it is not surprising that a special swan-upping (tagging) ceremony is held on the Thames in July. There is even an official Royal Master of

Windsor waterfowl

the Swans, who supervises the tagging of swans and cygnets. The swan upping on the Thames has become something of a tourist attraction, although the typical tourist may have trouble attending because the event moves along the river between the towns of Walton-on-Thames and Whitchurch.

The swans at Windsor are so-called mute swans; however, they are anything but mute, hissing and honking endlessly. The historical fuss over swan ownership was based on the fact that swans were once an important royal food group. If this situation had continued to the present day, the Windsor McDonald's might be serving McSwan sandwiches. Fortunately, swans are not on the menu, but they do add to the atmosphere along the Thames at Windsor.

Lego Invades Windsor

It is hard to ignore the fact that Legoland is only three miles down the road from Windsor. The intrusion of modern life on historic Windsor is epitomized by the Lego theme park.

Visitors can go from the 900-year-old stones of Windsor Castle to the new plastic bricks of Legoland Windsor in about ten minutes via a shuttle bus that departs from both Windsor rail stations. The question is: Do you want to? For children under age twelve who love to play with Legos, this theme park will probably be a big hit. Older children may be disappointed because much of the park is geared to younger kids. For example, the rides are pretty tame by modern theme park standards. But one ride for the younger set gives kids the chance to practice "driving" automobiles through an elaborate mock-up of city streets with traffic lights and signs. Chaos and fun ensue, especially for non-British children, who have to adjust to British traffic rules.

But the real jaw-dropping sights for the true Lego fan (and his or her parents) are the Star Wars scenes and the elaborate miniature European cities and landscapes built entirely from the plastic blocks. The model of London is phenomenal, although the cynic may point out the irony of paying to see a Lego model of London when the real thing is just a few miles away.

Legoland is a clean, well-run park designed to market the Lego brand, but don't expect free product giveaways or bargain-priced Legos for sale. Although the gift shop overflows with Lego merchandise, the prices are basically retail. In fact, some things cost more at Legoland than they do in toy stores.

True Lego fans can spend the night in the Legoland Windsor Resort Hotel, where the Lego theme carries over into the Lego pirate, kingdom, or adventure family bedrooms.

Where? When? £?

Legoland Windsor

Location: Windsor, about three miles from Windsor Castle

Transportation: Shuttle bus from Windsor's train stations

Address: Winkfield Road, Windsor, Berkshire SL4 4AY

Phone/email: 017 5362 6182/ Legoland.Enquiries@merlinentertainments.biz

Hours: The park is open from mid-March through early November, opening at 10:00 a.m. and closing between 5:00 and 7:00 p.m., depending on the season. Check the website for details.

Time needed: Two to four hours

Admission: Tickets are expensive, but there are discounts for children and seniors. Children under age three get in free. Discounted advance purchase tickets can be booked online.

Facilities: Many restaurants and snack bars on-site. Outdoor picnic spots. Toilets and baby-changing areas. Storage lockers and strollers (pushchairs) available for rent. Most areas are wheelchair accessible.

Website: www.legoland.co.uk

Off to Oxfordshire

Visitors to Windsor never really leave suburban London, but those who venture farther northwest to Oxfordshire can truly escape the city. Tourist agencies differ on where the heart of England lies, but if this is not quite England's heart, with Oxford University at its center, Oxfordshire may qualify as England's brain.

There are many reasons to visit. The city of Oxford and its university are obvious destinations. Oxfordshire is also known as a gateway to the undeniably quaint Cotswolds region, and Stratford-upon-Avon is just a few miles farther northwest. But because our goal is to give just a taste of the region, we will do that by describing two local attractions: the grandeur of Blenheim Palace and the mystery of the Rollright Stones.

Blenheim Palace

The year is 1704. What can a nobleman do to earn the absolute gratitude of England's Queen Anne? Why, defeat the French, of course. That's exactly what John Churchill did, and Blenheim Palace was his reward. Churchill, the first Duke of Marlborough, received the Royal Manor of Woodstock and the queen's promise to pay for the construction of Blenheim Palace. After falling out of royal favor, Churchill completed the palace at his own expense. In the years that followed, his descendants surrounded Blenheim with some of the country's most fantastic gardens.

If you spend much time traveling around Britain, grand palaces and stellar gardens become almost commonplace. But even to a veteran tourist, Blenheim Palace is something special. Gazing at the exterior of the palace, it's hard not to start humming the theme music from *Downton Abbey*. This is a palace of royal proportions, but it is also a private home. Inside, the grandeur and scale continue. The Long Library, for example, is one of the longest rooms in any private home in England. The library

Blenheim Palace

contains thousands of books and one heck of a sound system—a cathedral-sized pipe organ at the end of the vast room.

The Churchill name brings many visitors to Blenheim. The palace tour includes the room where Winston Churchill was born in 1874, and Churchill memorabilia and photographs are on display. This is an ideal location to explain to children the importance of Winston Churchill, perhaps linking the man to sites they have visited in London, such as the Churchill War Rooms. Kids may be interested to learn that Churchill's mother was an American and that Winston Churchill was one of only a handful of people to be granted honorary US citizenship. Churchill is buried in the nearby Oxfordshire town of Blanton.

The 2,100 acres of gardens and park that surround the palace are as impressive as the building itself. The gardens were designed by Lancelot "Capability" Brown, the architect of England's finest gardens. Blenheim Lake and the surrounding gardens are among Brown's top examples of landscape magic. Families can rent rowboats here or take a motor launch trip on the lake.

Blenheim is no relic; the palace is home to the current Duke of Marlborough and his family. Upkeep on the palace and the surrounding park is not cheap, so the duke opened part of the palace to tourists and added some attractions to entice visitors. The latter may seem unnecessary to adults who are interested in seeing the landscape artistry of Capability Brown or visiting the birthplace of Winston Churchill. But for kids, the duke's amusement park additions are great fun. So while you are touring the palace, promise your children a ride on the miniature train. While you are ogling the rose gardens, remind the kids that they'll get to go through the palace's maze. Younger children can romp in the adventure play area, and the craft studio is a good option on rainy days. Children and adults alike will be intrigued by the Blenheim Butterfly House, where exotic butterflies fly free.

WHERE? WHEN? £?

BLENHEIM PALACE

Location: Woodstock, eight miles north of Oxford on the A44 roadway (about sixty-five miles from London)

Transportation: Driving is more direct, but there is train service from Paddington station in London to Oxford, with a connecting bus to Blenheim Palace.

Address: Woodstock, Oxfordshire OX20 1PP

Phone/email: 0800 849 6500 (recorded info, UK calls only); 019 938 11091/operations@blenheimpalace.com

Hours: The palace is open daily from 10:30 a.m. to 5:30 p.m. from mid-February to the end of October. Open Wednesday through Sunday from November through early December. Last admission to the palace is 4:45 p.m. Formal gardens open 10:00 a.m. to 5:30 p.m. Pleasure garden open 10:00 a.m. to 6:00 p.m. Park hours are 9:00 a.m. to 6:00 p.m. (or dusk, if earlier).

Time needed: Three hours or longer

Admission: Tickets are moderately priced. There are discounts for children, students, seniors, and families. Parks/gardens-only tickets are available. Discounted advance purchase tickets available online.

Facilities: Restaurant, cafés, and picnic area on-site. Toilets and baby-changing areas. Some areas of the palace and grounds are not wheelchair accessible.

Website: www.blenheimpalace.com

In Search of Stones

Nearly everyone has heard of Stonehenge, but many foreign tourists may be surprised to find that Britain is dotted with other stone circles. Some circles are large and well-known, but many more are obscure structures lying in the middle of cow pastures. Although the major sites have been excavated, x-rayed, and studied by scholars, the smaller stone circles are explained best by local legends.

The Rollright Stones are located in pastureland near the tiny village of Long Compton, not far from the Oxfordshire town of Chipping Norton. On one trip, after taxing our map-reading skills, we managed to find this stone circle. The gatekeeper, in a tiny shack, charged our two children fifty pence admission, but he promised that they could get the money back if they correctly counted the number of stones in the circle.

Rollright Stones

The stone circle contains some very eroded stones and some that are nearly buried in the ground, and the actual number of stones was the subject of some debate. The children each reported different numbers to the gatekeeper, who informed them they were both wrong, but he still cheerfully refunded their fifty pence.

In the Oxfordshire fields, we heard several of the legends associated with the Rollright Stones. The best-known story is documented to at least the 1500s, so it is not something the locals recently made up at the village pub. (More likely they made it up at the pub 500 years ago.) A king and his men were traveling through the area on their way to conquer England. They were intercepted by a local witch, who made what seemed to be a great offer to the king:

> Seven long strides shalt thou take
> And if Long Compton thou canst see,
> King of England thou shalt be.

"Hot diggity," said the king as he strapped on his running shoes. No, that's wrong. What really happened was that the king strode confidently across the field shouting:

> Stick, stock, stone.
> As King of England I shall be known.

But the king did not count on the slight rise in the ground that blocked his view of Long Compton village. After the king took his seventh step, the witch laughed and crowed, "I'll get you my pretty, and your little dog too!" No, sorry for the confusion; these witch stories all sound alike. What she really said was:

> As Long Compton thou canst not see
> King of England thou shalt not be.
> Rise up stick and stand still stone
> For King of England thou shalt be none;
> Thou and thy men hoar stones shall be
> And I myself an eldern tree.

This was the witch's way of turning the king into the King Stone that stands across the road from the Rollright Stones and the king's men into the nearby Kings Men Stone Circle. And with the last line of the spell, the witch went into retirement as an elder tree.

If you visit a stone circle during the summer solstice—the longest day of the year—you may be confronted with a different kind of tourist. The first clue may be the large number of vintage Volkswagen minibuses parked nearby or the impromptu campsites scattered in surrounding fields. You won't confuse the solstice celebrators with other tourists: their clothing fashions lean toward 1960s-era counterculture and the occasional robe.

On one of our visits around the time of the summer solstice, we noticed a long line of No Parking signs and traffic cones along the road near an isolated stone circle. Two National Trust vans were parked on the road, and several uniformed men were milling about. We stopped to talk with them. Careful not to offend, the National Trust rangers admitted that they were present to guard against an influx of "alternative" visitors. The previous year, they told us, scads of people had arrived to celebrate the solstice, overrunning the site and causing damage. All we saw that day were a few standard tourists, although as we drove away from the stone circle, we saw a campsite with a handful of solstice seekers.

Thus began an interesting conversation as we parents tried to explain who these unusual-looking people were and why they were flocking to stone circles on the longest day of the year. The problem of solstice celebrations became so acute at Stonehenge that local authorities sometimes closed off the site entirely on the summer solstice; now they admit limited numbers of solstice celebrators.

WHERE? WHEN? £?

ROLLRIGHT STONES

Location: Off the A3400 road, between Chipping Norton and the village of Long Compton on the Warwickshire/Oxfordshire border, not far from Blenheim Palace and Oxford

Hours: Sunrise to sunset

Time needed: Thirty minutes to an hour

Admission: Ridiculously inexpensive

Facilities: None. Not wheelchair accessible.

Websites: www.rollrightstones.co.uk; www.english-heritage.org.uk/rollrightstones

Baby, You Can Drive My Car

There's a lot of British countryside within a relatively short drive from London. Although the prospect of driving on the left can be daunting for some visitors, it's well worth the effort.

Country Churches

When driving the back roads of rural Britain, allow time to stop and visit village churches, not necessarily as a religious experience but for the history and local flavor they impart. Churches were once the focal point of village life in Britain, and they all have a story to tell (usually explained in a twenty-pence brochure sold inside the church).

Gustav Holtz was the organist at the church in the tiny Cotswolds village of Wyck Rissington. He went on to fame as the composer of musical works such as *The Planets*. This historical side note was less fascinating to our children than the story of an elaborate maze formerly located near the village church. Fearing that the maze would be overrun by visitors, its builder razed the maze, and only a commemorative mosaic plaque remains on the church wall.

Church graveyards provide a resting place for the dead, but they can also serve as a temporary resting spot for the weary tourist. Ancient cemeteries are a good place to sit and absorb some of the quiet village atmosphere. The dead don't mind if you discreetly munch a picnic snack while sitting quietly on a cemetery bench, reading stone inscriptions and contemplating their lives.

You will find another type of religious site in British towns and countryside. Hundreds of abbeys and cathedrals stand in ruined glory throughout Britain, a legacy of religious strife in the country's history. Try to visit at least one of these interesting ruins. Visit too many, though, and kids may begin to complain, "Geez, *another* old wrecked church?"

Now that we've whetted your appetite for a field trip, it is time to review some practical matters about traveling around Britain.

Hit the Road

Unless you have the nerves of a big-city taxicab driver, don't even think of driving in London. But if you are planning an extended trip outside the city, consider renting a midsize car, minivan, or SUV for exploring Britain. Fitting family luggage in the trunk of a small car can be difficult, but in a larger vehicle, luggage fits and kids have more room. The visibility from a minivan or SUV is good enough that you might see over the hedgerows that border many of the rural roads. Of course, the convenience of a larger vehicle must be balanced against the fuel economy of a smaller car because fuel costs are high in Britain.

Car rental in Britain is not cheap, especially for family-sized vehicles. Consider arranging the rental online before leaving home because local rentals in Britain are sometimes more expensive than those made in advance. In addition to contacting major car rental companies directly, check with your airline and with online car rental brokers like AutoEurope. Before paying for optional collision insurance on a rental, contact your credit card company to see if coverage is automatically included when you charge the rental.

"Drive a car on the wrong side of the road? You've got to be kidding!" is a common reaction from non-British tourists heading to Britain. Generally, driving on the left is less of a challenge than you might imagine. It helps that the driver's seat is on the right, along with the appropriate controls. No, the gas and brake pedals are not reversed, but the gearshift is on the left, and that means shifting with your left hand, something that may overtax your coping skills. We recommend renting a car with automatic transmission, despite the extra cost.

Once on the road, repeat this mantra: keep left, keep LEFT, KEEP LEFT! Actually, this is not overly difficult, because everybody else is keeping left, too—just follow them. Maybe the most difficult maneuver is turning right at an intersection and remembering to head for the left lane as you get on the next road (keep left, keep LEFT . . .).

Traffic circles ("roundabouts" in Britspeak) are common, and there is a learning curve for the driving tourist. Yield to the traffic in the circle—it will be coming from your right—but once you are in the circle, yield to no one. In a multilane roundabout, the outside lane is for immediate exits and the inner lanes are for those continuing around the circle. Move left to exit out of the circle and use your turn signal to indicate whether you are turning out or staying in the roundabout. Miss your turnoff? Just keep going around the circle. Explaining this is harder than driving it, assuming you KEEP LEFT!

American tourist wreaking havoc on the byways of the UK

Driving in unfamiliar territory on the "wrong" side of the road is a lot easier if one person navigates while the other drives. Make sure you have good, detailed maps; carefully plan your routes in advance; and keep your sense of humor. Investing in (or renting) a GPS navigation system will certainly help, as will a smartphone or tablet device that uses cell phone signals to track progress on-screen using interactive maps.

As in any country, if you drive the superhighways you will miss much of the countryside and small towns. Britain's M roads are similar to American interstate highways, French autoroutes, and German autobahns. The more interesting routes are usually smaller A- or B-class roads, but you need good maps to negotiate the back roads. Where there's a choice, take the road that goes through an ancient village or requires a short ferryboat ride. You'll know that you're on the scenic route when the road is narrower than your driveway back home.

Time and Distance

Although England is a small country, we wonder sometimes if the English mile is the same unit of measurement as the North American mile. Miles don't mean much in cities, where distances are usually measured in blocks, but while driving in the English countryside, we once spotted a sign that read "Nottingham, nine miles." The town was not on our planned itinerary, but it seemed a reasonable detour because the children wanted to see Sherwood Forest. We got off the M superhighway and started along smaller roads toward Nottingham. We drove and drove, and drove some more before finally arriving in the legendary town about forty minutes later. We concluded that traveling those nine miles fully explains the origins of the phrase "around Robin Hood's barn."

"Miles? Isn't the United Kingdom on the metric system?" you may ask. Well, yes and no.

Road distances and speed limits are marked in miles, feet, inches, and other, mostly outmoded, units of measure. The lesson we learned after driving thousands of miles on British roads is that the distance in miles may be small, but so are many of the roads. Once you exit the major highways, it is driving time, not distance, that matters most in planning a trip. Always allow extra driving time for contingencies:

- Narrow, winding roads—our favorites in Cornwall were about ten feet wide (total, for both directions).

- Cattle and sheep crossings—livestock crossings are marked by flashing warning lights.

- Roadwork—even on the smallest backcountry roads, you will find work being done but no flagmen or flagwomen; Britons use portable traffic signals at both ends of a project to direct traffic.

- Gypsy caravans—real Gypsies, in colorful horse-drawn wagons, going three miles per hour in a no-passing zone. Gypsies are a rare sight in twenty-first-century Britain, but there are still a few *travelers* on the road. Consider yourself lucky if you see them, despite the traffic delay.

- Unmarked roads—tiny roads are usually signposted toward somewhere but may not have a route number.

- Farm traffic—nothing compares with following a fertilizer wagon for a few fragrant, winding miles.

Train Wizardry

Arriving at King's Cross rail station, Britain's most famous modern-day wizard was as confused as any London tourist. To catch the Hogwarts Express train, Harry Potter searched the station for the elusive, invisible platform 9¾. Although most Muggles won't face this problem, Harry's experience proves that it pays to know what you are doing before walking into a London rail station.

Trains let you add day trips to your visit, giving your family a chance to broaden its horizons beyond London proper without renting a car. Wonderful spots like Windsor and Hampton Court are less than an hour by train from London. In two hours, you can journey to the fascinating cities of Bath, Oxford, or York.

Rail travel works well with restless children because they can move around, look out the windows, amuse other passengers, get a snack, and visit the loo . . . without stopping or slowing down progress toward your destination. Here are some train travel trips:

- Round-trip tickets are called "return tickets" in Britain. For day trips outside London, advance purchase and "off-peak day return" fares are often the best deals.

- Rail passes, such as the Britrail Pass, can be a good deal for those planning extensive rail travel in the United Kingdom. For a few day trips out of London, a rail pass is not always necessary or economical. Note that many rail-cards issued in the United Kingdom are for UK residents only.

- Standard-class seats are usually sufficient, and first-class accommodations are not often worth the cost difference on short-distance rail journeys.

- Do a little homework and try to sit on the side of the train with the best view. For example, if you are traveling on a coastal railway, sit on the side facing the water.

- Seat reservations are a good idea on busy trains, and they are required on some routes. Tickets can be obtained and reservations can be made at major rail stations or online.

- Avoid the front rail cars ("coaches" or "carriages" in Brit-speak). Air pressure changes when entering tunnels can cause ear discomfort, particularly for young children.

- Some train cars are set up with four facing seats and a table between. Reserve one of these so young kids can read, play games, or eat a snack and you can keep tabs on them. But don't sit here if no one wants to ride facing backward.

- Seat reservations may be displayed on screens above the seats. The conductor (ticket inspector) may stick a ticket on top of the seatback to mark it as taken. Check that you are not sitting in someone else's seat!

- On some trains, you can sit in quiet coaches where mobile phones and audible music are banned. Children are allowed, but noisy kids may elicit scowls.

- Some rail stations don't have lifts (elevators). If family members can't carry luggage up and down stairs, then you face a challenge. Most stations have luggage carts but no porters, and carts are useless on stairways. Allow plenty of extra time to lug that luggage or risk missing a train.

- In London, the main rail stations are all on one level or they have lifts, so luggage toting is not a big problem. However, some London Underground/Tube stations do not have lifts or escalators.

- Some smaller stations in the countryside are fully auto-mated, with electronic ticket vending machines and com-puter screens that announce arrivals and departures. This can be disconcerting to the tourist whose inclination is to look for an information counter to ask questions. With a little practice, and adequate time before your train departs, the automated system works well.

- Automated ticket machines may not function for trav-elers without chip-and-pin credit cards (see the "Money Matters" section).

- Train travel is a picnic opportunity; the food served on trains is medicore, and it can be expensive.

- British railway employees sometimes go on strike, disrupting rail service. That's a real problem for the tourist who has to get around on a schedule and can't just hop into the family automobile if the trains are not running. However, the rail strikes are usually scheduled for specific days so travelers can plan around them.

Rail Station Roulette

When railway travel got its start in Britain, London responded by building rail stations—lots of them—all over the city. There's no Grand Central Station in London. Instead, the traveler is faced with more than a dozen major train stations scattered around town. Like the spokes on a wheel, the rail lines from each station reach out and serve different parts of Britain. Major stations include:

- Paddington
- Marylebone
- Euston
- St. Pancras International
- King's Cross
- Liverpool Street
- Fenchurch Street
- Blackfriars
- Charing Cross
- Stratford
- Cannon Street
- London Bridge
- Waterloo and Waterloo East
- Victoria

With the exception of St. Pancras and King's Cross, which are right across the street from each other, getting from one station to another can be a pain. The Tube is not practical if you're carrying much luggage. London's bus system indirectly connects rail stations, but this is not ideal either. Taxis are probably the most feasible, if expensive, way to get between rail stations in London. Try to avoid rush hours because whatever conveyance you choose—bus, taxi, or Tube—getting around town takes longer when London's streets are jammed.

Does train travel to and from London sound like a nightmare? Fortunately, most tourists will probably use only one or two rail stations, either to get into London from an airport or to take a day trip outside the city. The table on page 194 shows examples of popular rail destinations, some of the London stations that serve them, and the approximate journey time. Remember, rail services change, so check the official National Rail website at www.nationalrail.co.uk before committing yourself to a trip.

Paddington Bear at Paddington station

Harry Potter fans know that the Hogwarts Express departs from platform 9¾ inside King's Cross station. But crowds of movie fans caused problems for train travelers, so King's Cross officials created a faux platform 9¾ just outside the station near platform 1. Scenes from Harry Potter movies were filmed in the interior of the main station; the exterior station shots were made at St. Pancras station, across the street from King's Cross. To take a tour of the studios where the Harry Potter films were produced, walk a half-mile east and board a train at Euston rail station for the twenty-minute trip north to Watford Junction and the nearby Warner Brothers Studio Tour (www.wbstudiotour.co.uk).

Destination	Train leaves from	Travel time
Gatwick Airport	Victoria or London Bridge	30 minutes
Heathrow Airport	Paddington	15 minutes
Bath	Paddington	90 minutes
Windsor	Paddington or Waterloo	45 minutes
Paris	St. Pancras International	3 hours
Cambridge	King's Cross or Liverpool Street	1 hour
York	King's Cross	2 hours
Edinburgh	King's Cross	4.5 hours
Hogwarts	King's Cross	All day

Train Times and Tickets

Tickets can be purchased at rail stations, or even once you are on board, but advance planning will save you time and money. For schedules, station information, and purchases, visit the National Rail website (www.nationalrail.co.uk). This site provides links to railway operating companies, updates on schedule disruptions, locations of rail stations, and other information. For information on train travel between continental Europe and Britain, visit the Eurostar website (www.eurostar.com).

PART FOUR

Stop Dreaming, Start Planning

When to Go?
Method to Your Trip-Planning Madness
Finding a Hotel
Food, Glorious Food

When to Go?

Don't you just love this section in the typical guidebook? Parents with school-age children generally *can't* go to London in September or October even though the weather may be beautiful. And most kids would throw a fit if you decided to pack up and go to London for Christmas or another important holiday: "What about the presents? How will Santa Claus find me?" So yes, it's great to contemplate going at some other time of year, but most families will travel during the months of June, July, or August.

Now that you've had a reality check, is there any way for overseas visitors to travel in the summer but avoid the crowds? One tip is to plan around the times when British schools are on summer break. British schools usually get out for the summer in early to mid-July, whereas North American school years generally end in June, giving American families a window of opportunity for travel. During this period, you will still encounter crowds, but likely not the crush that can occur during summer school holidays. Crowding in London during the summer is usually caused by foreign tourists who swarm into the city in August, when many Londoners are out of the city on vacation.

Visitors to London will feel the midsummer crunch on the plane trip over, at the airport (clearing customs and immigration lines can take quite a while), and at major tourist attractions in the city (lines to see the crown jewels are notorious).

Some airlines hike fares for summer travel beginning on or about June 15, so those who can begin a trip before the rates go up may save on airfare. On the other hand, airlines sometimes offer summer fare sales, often announcing them in April or later. This can be a dilemma: wait too long and all the June flights will be filled; book too early and risk missing a summer sale. But with today's air travel market, predictability of fares is almost a thing of the past.

Rates at hotels that cater primarily to business travelers don't necessarily increase in summer. In fact, families may find summer price breaks at London's business hotels. Weekend rates at business hotels can also be relatively low. That's a good thing, because London hotel rates are expensive by any standard.

Holidays

Here's a list of the major public holidays observed in Britain:

- New Year's Day—January 1; if the date falls on a weekend, the bank holiday is the next weekday
- Good Friday—varies
- Easter Monday—varies
- Early May Bank Holiday—first Monday in May
- Spring Bank Holiday—last Monday in May
- Summer Bank Holiday—last Monday in August
- Christmas Day—December 25; if the date falls on a weekend, the bank holiday is the next weekday after Boxing Day
- Boxing Day—December 26

London ice-skaters in December

Bank holiday is a quaint term designating an official holiday when banks and some places of business are closed. Be sure to check whether the tourist attractions you want to visit are open on a holiday. Many are closed around Christmas and New Year's, but open on other holidays.

Weather

Britain in summertime means that you can expect the following weather conditions: warm, hot, cool, cold, sunny, cloudy, and wet. Sometimes these all occur in one day! Here's a table showing average high and low temperatures by month in London:

Month	Average low	Average high
January	36° F / 2° C	46° F / 8° C
February	36° F / 2° C	47° F / 9° C
March	39° F / 4° C	52° F / 11° C
April	41° F / 5° C	56° F / 13° C
May	46° F / 8° C	63° F / 17° C
June	52° F / 11° C	69° F / 21° C
July	57° F / 14° C	73° F / 23° C
August	56° F / 13° C	73° F / 23° C
September	52° F / 11° C	67° F / 19° C
October	46° F / 8° C	59° F / 15° C
November	41° F / 5° C	52° F / 11° C
December	38° F / 3° C	48° F / 9° C

Average temperatures are derived from years of actual data, so you could experience a hot or cold spell during the relatively few days of your visit regardless of the averages. Use the averages as a guide, but pack something to wear if you encounter abnormal temperatures. There has been a recent trend toward summer heat waves in London and southern England as global climate changes affect Britain.

A bonus to traveling in June is that as the summer solstice approaches, the days get long—really long—at this latitude. Twilight lasts well past 10:00 p.m. in London; as you travel north to the English Lake District or Scotland, there is light in the western sky at 11:30 p.m. This gives the summer tourist extra hours of sightseeing time. The longer days don't necessarily mean extended opening times for tourist attractions, but you can use the longer daylight hours for outdoor activities. British Summer Time (daylight savings time) starts on the last Sunday of March and ends on the last Sunday of October. Implementing year-round BST is under consideration.

A Method to Your Trip-Planning Madness

It is amazing how many families do almost no research before taking a significant trip. At times, this method works fine, but serendipitous tourists may miss some great experiences simply because they did not have enough information before arriving in London.

A solution? If you have the luxury of time, start planning six months or more before a trip. Buy or borrow every guidebook you can find (borrow others, *buy* this one). Consider letting your children help plan the trip. Divide the books among family members and start reading. Take notes about things of interest, then swap books and take more notes. Go online and search for sites related to travel, tourism, dining, events, and lodging in London. Browse VisitLondon.com, the city's tourism website, for information.

Give kids a map and let them mark sites, hotels, and points of interest. In the time leading up to a trip, point out news about London in newspapers, online, and on television. Mention some historical connections to London and how these are related to subjects that children have studied in school. Encourage kids to read some British children's literature, especially stories that take place in areas you will visit.

When you and your children cannot read another guidebook, website, Sherlock Holmes or Paddington Bear story, it's time for a family conference. Everyone can contribute from their notes as the family begins to develop a master list of places and things to see and do and some ideas of where to stay. Narrowing your list down to a trip plan is step two—and this is no small challenge. At this point, independent travelers will begin contacting airlines and hotels directly. People who find this prospect too daunting may decide it's time to "punt" and turn to a travel agent for help.

Travel Agents and Trip Insurance

If you are using a travel agent, be sure to pick one with extensive, recent travel experience in London. Any travel agent can sell packaged tours, but it takes knowledge for an agent to answer questions about specific hotels, activities, and other aspects of a trip. Beware of anyone—travel agent or guidebook writer—who strongly steers you toward a particular hotel (or airline, car rental agency, and the like). They could be providing their best impartial, factual advice, or an ulterior economic motive may be driving the recommendation.

It is wise to use agents who are members of such groups as the American Society of Travel Agents (US), the Association of British Travel Agents (UK), the Association of Canadian Travel Agencies (Canada), or similar organizations. These groups promote ethics in the industry and provide travelers with recourse if they have a complaint about member agents.

Travel/trip insurance is an option to consider when planning a vacation, with or without a travel agent. Keep in mind that trip insurance has its limitations, often buried in pages of small print, and adds to the cost of a vacation. Insurance can be purchased as part of a travel package or independently.

Laying Out an Itinerary — The Block Planning Method

You've read extensively, taken copious notes, and bookmarked lots of Internet sites. Brochures and guidebooks are piled on the dining room table and filling up your e-book reader. How to organize all this information into a trip plan? Our suggestion is to use what we call the block planning method. Lay out the days of the trip in calendar form, with room to list events and places to visit. Take the family's "want to do" list and start blocking out a possible itinerary on the calendar.

Here are some ideas to keep in mind as you plan your itinerary:

- First, fill in anything that is fixed, such as arrival and departure dates and times. If you have prepurchased theater tickets, fill in the show times on the calendar. Add any special one-time events you wish to attend.

- Plan for variety by mixing and matching types of activities. Don't put all the museums on one day and all the parks on another. The wise parent carefully intersperses kid-friendly activities with the more adult (possibly kid-boring) events.

- Allow plenty of time for each location or activity. Our suggestions about how long you might want to spend at certain places are just estimates. You may want to devote more or less time at any spot, but when planning, err on the side of leaving extra time. And remember, it takes time to get from place to place.

- Consider geography. Arrange the days logically, grouping places and events that are reasonably close together on the same day. Plot the itinerary on a map; if routes between sites look like a web spun by a drunken spider, you may want to rearrange your plans.

- Be flexible. Have some backup ideas in case it rains on the day you plan to visit a park or if the lines at some popular destinations are too long.

- Be realistic. As a rule of thumb, when traveling with children, a family can do three major activities a day: one each in the morning, afternoon, and evening. Much more than that and you risk exhausting your kids— and yourself!

Planning the itinerary graphically is the best way we know to get a handle on the family plan. Of course, once something's written down on paper, or in an online calendar, you'll probably change it several times before leaving for London (and several times once you are there).

Don't Leave Home without the Book

As your plans firm up, we suggest creating a three-ring notebook or portfolio that includes:

- A printout of your block plan itinerary
- Copies of the photograph page from passports (if you lose a passport, the copy will speed up the replacement time)
- Printouts of hotel reservation confirmations
- Copies of airline tickets, theater tickets, museum passes, rental car reservations
- Phone numbers to report lost credit cards
- Copies or printouts of a few pages from those huge guidebooks that you don't want to lug around Britain. Two suggestions: copy only pages from books you own and use the copies only for personal use while on the trip. Of course, if you have an e-book reader or computer with you, you can bring along electronic versions of many guides.

A notebook is the traditional way to organize, but all the information can easily be replicated on a tablet computer, laptop, or smartphone.

Just how valuable is "the Book"? It has saved our vacation when we were faced with a balky hotel, airline, or car rental reservation. If you encounter "Sorry, we have no record of that low rate" or "We never promised a vehicle with automatic transmission," you can reply, "Well, as you can see from my copy of your email confirmation here . . ." as you show them the documentation from the Book.

Events

Events, big and small, planned and serendipitous, can make a trip special. Your goal as an intrepid tourist is to take advantage of special events that you know about in advance and to be flexible enough to enjoy those unplanned moments when events find you.

On one trip, we had arranged far in advance for tickets to the Ceremony of the Keys at the Tower of London. What we didn't know until we arrived in London was that we were attending the ceremony on the same night as a celebration at nearby Tower Bridge. After the solemn keys ceremony, we ran to the Thames embankment and watched spectacular fireworks above Tower Bridge. That was serendipity at its best.

Seasonal events can enhance your family's London experience. In the warm weather months, concerts in parks and other outdoor events abound. But Londoners don't completely retreat inside during the winter. Temporary ice-skating rinks pop up around the city from November through January, and lights and decorations along major shopping streets draw shoppers and tourists outside.

The publication *Time Out London* has up-to-date information on events and activities. Printed copies are available at London newsstands and in bookstores; there are also digital editions and apps.

Finding a Hotel

"Going to London?" said the strange boy, when Oliver had concluded.
"Yes."
"Got any lodgings?"
"No."
"Money?"
"No."
The strange boy whistled; and put his arms into his pockets as far as the
big coat sleeves would let them go.
"Don't fret your eyelids on that score," said the young gentleman.
—*Oliver Twist*, by Charles Dickens

When considering where to stay in London, check as many sources as possible. Read through guidebooks and surf websites to locate accommodations in central London. Find a great place? What does the AA (British Automobile Association) guide or website say? Is the same hotel listed in the Michelin Guide or any of the numerous lodging guides covering London? Go online again and see what people are saying on travel message boards or services like TripAdvisor.com. Hotel websites are biased, but they provide photographs of the hotel, maps showing its exact location, and other useful information. Remember, a "palace" to one person may be a "pigsty" to someone else. Do not rely on any one source when deciding where to stay, lest you end up sleeping in a pigsty, or worse.

Even with many sources of information, families traveling to London face several challenges in finding suitable lodging. We have some suggestions, but no outright solutions, to finding:

- Family accommodations
- A quiet, comfortable place to stay
- A convenient location
- Something you can afford

Family Rooms

The typical North American hotel room contains two double/ queen beds, a full bathroom, and air-conditioning. A family of two adults and one or two children can usually fit into this con-figuration, perhaps with a rollaway bed for one child. It's not par-adise, especially for the parents, but it suffices. For a few dollars more, a traveling family can stay at an all-suite hotel chain in relative comfort and privacy.

This model rarely applies to London's hotel industry; it is sometimes difficult to find modern family accommodations in the city. One possibility is to try a familiar brand hotel such as a Holiday Inn, Hilton, or Marriott. Kids sometimes stay free with their parents in a typical, modern-style hotel room. Some budget-minded hotel chains, such as Premier Inn and Holiday Inn Express, also offer North American–style accommodations in London. But even at brand-name hotels, make no assumptions. Check with the individual hotel before making a reservation.

A nice little hotel in London

Take a moment to learn the euphemisms employed in the British hotel industry. "Traditional" often means old, a "tourist class hotel" is a lower-grade property, and "first class" is not necessarily top of the line. Modifiers are sometimes used to denote middle-range hotels, so you may see a "moderate first-class" hotel or a "superior tourist class" property.

Triple, quad, or family rooms do exist in London hotels, but they are hard to find. Add other seemingly reasonable criteria, such as air-conditioning or a central location, are even more rare. In a traditional tourist-class or moderate first-class hotel, a family room is likely to be a double bed and two single beds in a slightly-larger-than-normal hotel room.

In the moderately priced London hotel scene, the Premier Inn hotel chain has expanded into central London, offering reasonably priced hotels downtown. Premier Inn hotels feature modern, non-smoking rooms, including some family bedrooms. Some Premier Inns do not have air-conditioning, however. Premier Inn's corporate strategy is to become the largest hotel chain in London, so there are Premier Inns across the city, including properties at County Hall next to the London Eye, near Tower Bridge, and adjacent to Victoria rail station. Premier Inn and its competitors are making inroads into the tourist trade at the expense of older, traditional London hotels. Hotels built for the 2012 London Olympics have also increased lodging opportunities in the city.

Quiet, Please

Even though finding an air-conditioned hotel in London is sometimes a challenge, your family will probably want air-conditioning during a summer visit. Not because London is usually hot in summer, but at times it can be. The reason for air-conditioning is noise control. London is a very busy city, and closed windows keep out (some) noise. In warm weather, without air-conditioning, the hotel guest is faced with a choice of no sleep because the street outside is so loud or no sleep because the room is stuffy and warm.

The need for quiet is one reason to check out the newer hotel chains. Their construction tends to include double-glazed windows, carpeting, some sound insulation, and quieter plumbing. Remember to double-check about air-conditioning.

Our preference for modern, air-conditioned hotels may not be yours. If you prefer small, older hotels or B&Bs, you may be able to find something suitable, but it will take some research. Sometimes lodging guidebooks associate "quiet" with "no children allowed." For families, quiet means the possibility of a good night's sleep, not the quiet of a nursing home. Of course, nothing guarantees a quiet hotel or B&B. Ever notice that other hotel guests seem to practice slamming their room doors after 11:00 p.m.? It is these same people who think that a hotel hallway is a fine place to hold loud, protracted conversations late at night or first thing in the morning.

If you locate a prospective hotel on a large-scale London map, you might get a clue about potential noise from road traffic. A hotel facing busy Piccadilly or Kensington Road is going to be exposed to more traffic noise than some place a block off the main artery. No guarantees here, because the hotel could be right next to the Party All Night Pub or some equally loud venue. Google Maps' street view is a good way to take a virtual stroll around the neighborhood before booking a hotel.

Unfortunately, there may be an inverse relationship between a quiet hotel and one with a central location.

Location, Location, Location

London has good public transportation, so getting from a distant hotel to the major tourist attractions is certainly possible. But do you really want to spend valuable vacation time traveling on the Tube, with children in tow, during the morning or evening rush hour? If your budget allows, wouldn't it be better to stay near some of the sites you want to see?

This distinction escapes many experts who advise tourists to look for reasonably priced lodgings that cluster in some remote areas of London. Before deciding on a specific hotel, take a tour of some of the city's neighborhoods. Read on to learn about the kinds of lodging to expect, some pros and cons of staying in each spot, and how convenient the neighborhoods are to the major tourist sites.

Find **Buckingham Palace** near the middle of the map. The palace serves as the center point in the following description of the

London Neighborhoods

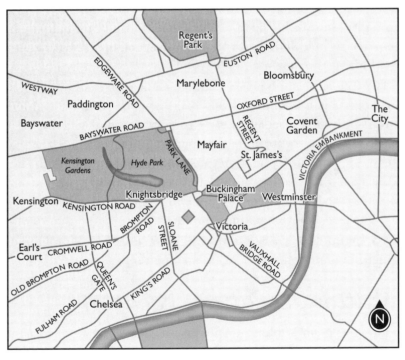

city's regions. The overview starts in the **Paddington/Bayswater** area northwest of Buckingham Palace. Paddington and Bayswater are home to lots of lower-cost hotels, including many tourist-class accommodations used by tour operators. There are also some midrange properties, such as a Doubletree Hotel and a Hilton along Bayswater Road. Bayswater is known for its multicultural restaurants and shops, but some of this area is far from major tourist sites, so visitors must rely on public transportation.

One advantage of the Paddington/Bayswater area is its convenience for people arriving and departing from Heathrow Airport. The Paddington rail station is the London terminus for the Heathrow Express and Heathrow Connect train services. If rail transportation to the airport is critical, consider the Hilton Hotel connected to Paddington rail station. At the southern edge of this area, busy Bayswater Road runs along the top of Kensington Gardens and Hyde Park. Popular Notting Hill is just west of Bayswater.

South of Paddington/Bayswater is **South Kensington** and **Knightsbridge**. This region has hotels of all levels and is convenient for visiting Kensington Palace and Gardens as well as the Science, Natural History, and Victoria and Albert museums. Kensington Road is extremely busy (with accompanying traffic noise), but there are hotels on some quieter side streets, such as the four-star Millennium London Gloucester Hotel.

South and west of Kensington/Knightsbridge is **Earl's Court**, a neighborhood with a cluster of midpriced lodgings. These are popular places for tour companies to book budget travelers, and the quality varies. But Earl's Court is farther away from most tourist sites than Bayswater.

Trendy **Chelsea** is south of Knightsbridge and closer to Buckingham Palace than to Earl's Court. This area is home to many B&Bs, some large expensive hotels, and some high-end boutique properties. The five-star Draycott Hotel is an example of Chelsea's small top-tier hotels. Families interested in renting a short-term apartment/flat might consider Chelsea. Lovely as it is, Chelsea attracts young, affluent residents, but few major tourist sites are located here.

Victoria rail station is just south of Buckingham Palace, and **Victoria** is within walking distance of the palace and many other central sites. This neighborhood includes grimy locations as well as nicer spots, so choose carefully. The Goring, a small luxury hotel, is a fashionable choice for families with deep pockets. Rubens at the Palace is another popular hotel in this area, and there's a budget-level Premier Inn nearby.

The Westminster Abbey area is east of Buckingham Palace. Unfortunately, there are relatively few affordable hotels in this part of **Westminster**. It would be nice to stay so close to the abbey, Parliament, and other interesting locations, but real estate here is costly, and so are many of the hotels. One exception is the moderately priced Sanctuary House Hotel just south of St. James's Park. The upscale InterContinental Westminster and St. Ermine's hotels are nearby. Across the river from Parliament and next door to the London Eye, you'll find a moderately priced Premier Inn along with a swanky Marriott.

Slightly north of Westminster Abbey, and within walking distance of Buckingham Palace, is the ritzy **St. James's** area. The hotels in this area are among the most expensive in the city. The luxury Sofitel St. James's is in one of London's prime locations. The Stafford Hotel is tucked into a quiet St. James's side street and offers posh accommodations befitting the area. St. James's is often lumped with Mayfair, its northern neighbor, as a locale for upscale accommodations.

You can't get much more convenient than **Mayfair**, but convenience comes at a price. Many of the hotels, shops, and restaurants here are very expensive. Legendary hotels like Brown's, Claridge's, and the Dorchester call Mayfair home. There are a few chain hotels with reasonably priced rooms, although these are still expensive, just not outrageously so. A popular midrange choice is the Holiday Inn Mayfair, across the street from the over-the-top luxury of the Ritz. A few blocks north, the Chesterfield Mayfair Hotel offers luxury, although not at Ritz levels or prices.

East of Mayfair is the **Covent Garden** area. This neighborhood is close to West End theaters and attractions around Covent Garden Market. Theaters and the festival atmosphere of Covent

Garden generate much traffic and late-night noise. There aren't many hotels overlooking Covent Garden Market, but the popular Fielding Hotel is nearby, and the top-ranked Savoy is a five-minute walk away.

East of Covent Garden is **the City** and a group of tourist destinations, including St. Paul's Cathedral, the Tower of London, and Tower Bridge. The City is across the river from the Globe Theatre and other South Bank sites. Although the City is primarily a financial district, it does boast a number of hotels within walking distance of tourist sites that may be worth considering. There is a midrange Club Quarters near St. Paul's and a Novotel north of the Tower of London. Some new hotels have been built south of the Thames near the Tower, including a budget-level Premier Inn on Tower Bridge Road and a modern Hilton on Tooley Street.

Off the map and east of the City, hotels have sprung up in Canary Wharf and East London concurrent with redevelopment in these areas. Hotels in this area can be less expensive, except during special events. The ExCel exhibition center, near London City Airport, is surrounded by midlevel hotels, including offerings from Premier Inn, Novotel, Ibis, and the modern Aloft.

North of Covent Garden is **Bloomsbury**. Bloomsbury is near the British Museum, but not much else on the typical tourist's agenda. Although it may be too far to walk from here to many of London's central sites, Bloomsbury offers a number of hotels such as the midpriced Radisson Edwardian and the upscale Montague on the Gardens (both near the British Museum).

At the northern edge of the map is **Regent's Park**, close to the London Zoo, Regent's Canal, and a few tourist sites, but you'll need to take a Tube or taxi to get to the center of London from here. South of Regent's Park is the **Marylebone** area. The luxurious Langham Hotel and the exclusive Chiltern Firehouse Hotel are in Marylebone, along with a plethora of other properties. Marylebone is convenient to shopping along Oxford Street, and it has good access to the Tube, but it's a long walk to central London tourist attractions.

Anyone who has a late-night arrival or an early-morning departure from Heathrow or Gatwick Airport might consider staying at an airport hotel rather than making the commute to and from town. A high-end Sofitel is attached to Heathrow's Terminal 5, ultraconvenient for British Airways transatlantic flights. Heathrow's Terminal 4 has a Hilton, and, for those who aren't claustrophobic, there is a Yotel short-term "capsule hotel." At Gatwick Airport's south terminal, there is a BLOC Hotel, a Hilton, and another diminutive Yotel. The north terminal boasts a Hampton, a Sofitel, and a Premier Inn. Other properties that call themselves "airport hotels" are not actually at an airport and require shuttle bus rides from the terminals.

And That Will Be £350, Plus VAT and Service Charges

We promised to address four issues at the start of this section, and we've delivered on the first three: we've discussed finding family accommodations, given some hints on getting a quiet hotel room, and provided an overview of hotel locations. About the last issue—finding affordable places to stay—can we get back to you on that?

Seriously, it is tempting to skip this subject because of one simple fact: lodging in London is expensive. Lodging that meets all the criteria we have outlined is both difficult to find and expensive. There are no magic answers, but here are some suggestions.

Never Say Never

First, wherever you travel, never accept the published hotel rate at a large city hotel. You will always qualify for some lower rate: weekend packages, honeymoon packages (kind of hard to explain when you're traveling with kids, but worth a try), government rates, corporate rates, automobile association rates, senior citizen rates, advance purchase rates, special rates for people paying with a particular credit card . . . *something*. If nothing else works and you are planning to stay at a chain hotel, at least collect points by joining the chain's frequent-guest program.

Major hotel chains rely heavily on travelers booking through the Internet, but hotel websites aren't always perfect. Hotel chains also have toll-free telephone reservations numbers, but operators may be woefully uninformed about the details of their London properties. We've been told by a reservation service that a London hotel has no family rooms, only to call the hotel directly to find out that family rooms are available. Ask the operator to contact the hotel directly about family rooms if nothing appears in the reservations computer system. Much depends on the helpfulness and persistence of any individual reservations agent. We were lucky to work with one agent for a large hotel chain who negotiated two adjoining rooms at a discounted rate even though the chain's computer system did not include rates for family accommodations.

Like most large cities, London has many hotels that cater primarily to business travelers; these hotels may have lower rates on weekends than during the week. Although you will likely stay longer than a weekend, make sure to get the lower rate for at least the weekend portion of your stay. You can also take advantage of off-peak months at business-oriented London hotels. Happily, off-peak for business travel includes July and August, which is exactly when many families visit London on vacation.

Call Around

Sometimes it is possible to find low rates by calling a hotel directly. Take this a step further and compare rates quoted by the hotels, their corporate reservations centers, and websites. Bidding on a travel auction site is another way to obtain lower-cost accommodations, but travel auctions are not for everyone. It can be difficult to arrange family rooms, adjoining rooms, or any special configurations via an auction.

A word of caution: Be sure to compare apples to apples. Are the rooms the same? Some hotels have several grades of accommodations, including both recently refurbished rooms and shabby rooms. Does the quoted rate include:

- Value added tax (it should)
- Service charges
- Breakfasts or any meals (for the whole family or just two adults)

Make sure that the rates are quoted on the same basis: per room, per night. Do children stay free? If so, are there age limits? Finally, understand whether the rate is quoted in pounds, dollars, or euros. This advice sounds basic, but nasty surprises may await tourists who neglect to determine this information in advance.

Quality Ratings

Sherlock Holmes would have been comfortable searching for a decent place to stay in London, applying his powers of inductive reasoning, using his able assistant Watson, and examining clues under a magnifying glass. Holmes would have made a terrific trip planner because he seemed to have a lot of free time and no money worries.

Fortunately, someone has done a lot of detective work already. England's official tourist organization (Visit England) and one of its largest travel organizations (the Automobile Association, or AA) rate thousands of hotels, B&Bs, and other lodging establishments using a ratings system that awards one to five stars based on standards of quality, services offered, and facilities.

Generally, the more stars, the better the hotel or B&B, but there are differences. A hotel is graded with an emphasis on its facilities—for example, bathrooms, elevators, and room service. To qualify for one star, a hotel must have at least five guest rooms, offer all en suite or private baths, employ on-site staff, have adequate liability insurance, and so forth. Two-star hotels must offer all these amenities and hit a higher quality standard. At the three-star level, things like room service and public area Wi-Fi show up (although in-room Wi-Fi is required only for a four-star rating).

Amazingly, though, only five-star hotels are expected to offer air-conditioned rooms. As for toting your suitcases to your room, even a one-star hotel must offer help with luggage, although lifts/elevators to all floors are not required until the five-star level. Even around-the-clock hot water isn't required to qualify for a two-star hotel rating in Britain.

From a North American perspective, where inexpensive hotels usually come with air-conditioning and elevators, it's a little disconcerting to read these standards. "No hot water after 10:00 p.m.?" Well, tourist, you're not in Kansas anymore.

For B&Bs and other nonhotels, the star ratings differ a bit. For example, at the four-star level, at least half of a B&B's rooms must have private baths. A five-star B&B must provide fans in guest rooms on request during hot weather. With these standards at the upper end, it doesn't take much to imagine the potential of one-, two-, and three-star establishments.

To further qualify the ratings, the AA provides percentage scores, red-star "inspectors' choice" hotel awards, and gold stars for the best B&Bs. Finally, there are distinctions between types of hotels rated: large full-service hotels; quiet country house hotels; small hotels with less than twenty rooms and limited services; urban town house hotels with up to fifty high-quality rooms serving dinner or providing room service; and metro hotels with all hotel services except dinner.

Clearly, the simplified standards are not as simple as they appear.

Take the ratings systems with a grain of salt. One of the nicest places we stayed in Britain was a beautiful B&B in the tiny west coast village of Crackington Haven. The owners had dropped out of the official inspection program, claiming that it emphasized facilities at the expense of quality. They felt that although all visitors may want heat and hot water, not everyone needs all the amenities that garner a top rating.

The Flat Alternative

Families staying in London for more than a few days may want to consider letting a flat (renting an apartment) as an alternative to staying in a hotel. Flats come in all sizes and quality levels, and the better ones can cost every bit as much as a good hotel room. What a flat offers families is more space, perhaps even separate rooms for children and adults, and kitchen facilities in which to prepare meals. Groceries in London are not cheap, but fixing a few family meals in a flat is still less expensive than eating every meal in a restaurant.

Many rental flats are located in residential areas away from major tourist sites. If the flat is reasonably close to a Tube or suburban rail station, you will be able to commute to central London fairly easily, but this does add commuting logistics to a visit. Finding a quiet, comfortable flat may take more research than finding a suitable hotel room. Some factors to consider:

- Is this a legitimate rental and is the landlord/rental company reputable?
- Is a deposit required? How will you make payment?
- Is the flat air-conditioned?
- Is the building new, renovated, or "classic"?
- On what floor is the flat located? (In Britain, as in much of Europe, floors are labeled ground, first, second, etc., so a British first floor is an American second floor.)
- Are there lifts (elevators)?
- How convenient is the flat to what you want to see in London? Is it near a Tube stop?
- What is the neighborhood like?
- Is there a grocery store nearby?

Online rental services such as Airbnb and HomeAway have changed the face of the short-term rental market in London and elsewhere. There are also other more traditional companies specializing in London flat rentals. Renting a flat while on vacation is often a lifestyle choice. Do you want to mingle with the natives, shop for food, and fix meals? Do you have the time to devote to domestic chores during your visit?

My House Is Your House

Interesting conundrum: your family is headed to London, likely leaving your home empty during the trip. At the same time, a family in London might well be winging its way toward your hometown, leaving its London home vacant. The financial appeal of house swapping is patently obvious; only logistics stand in the way. That's where house-swapping services come into play. There are a number of international home exchange companies, including several based in London. Ask friends or look online to discover options that work best for your family.

Bodysgallen Hall, a country house hotel in north Wales

B&Bs, Country House Hotels, and Inns

Families traveling outside London may have an easier time finding a quiet, comfortable, affordable place to stay than those staying inside the city. There are many options: B&Bs, country house hotels, inns, traditional hotels, and modern chain hotels.

You can't go far in Britain without seeing a B&B. In central London, individual B&Bs are less common, but they do exist. The term *bed and breakfast* covers a lot of ground. It applies both to families that rent out one or two bedrooms in their homes and to larger establishments that are essentially small hotels. But virtually all B&Bs share one characteristic: the ubiquitous English breakfast (see the "Food, Glorious Food" section).

Country house hotels are a cross between a rural B&B and a hotel. Country house hotels often have more rooms than B&Bs, and they are usually upscale establishments. Because country house hotels are located in the countryside, most visitors to London will not stay in a country house hotel unless they are willing to stay far outside the city and commute in by train.

The term *inn* often implies a small establishment that rents rooms and has a restaurant that is open to nonresidents. In some cases, the presence of a pub or a restaurant can add an element of noise, as diners arrive, eat, drink, and are merry late into the night. Most inns are located in smaller towns and villages; they are not common in London.

The quality of B&Bs, country house hotels, and inns varies from simple to luxurious. Charm, a more subjective factor, also varies from "working-class spare bedroom" to "country squire's guest villa." It takes some detective work to determine an establishment's charm factor sight unseen. The process is like finding a hotel in London: get hold of as many guidebooks as you can, check multiple online sites, and cross-check ratings and evaluations. Social media and sites like TripAdvisor can be helpful, but beware of falsified reviews.

One debate among travelers in Britain is whether to reserve B&B rooms in advance or simply to find them as you travel from place to place. With children in tow, finding suitable accommodations can be challenging. A traveling family can't be as flexible as traveling adults because children may need beds in the same room with parents (or nearby). Add the fact that not all B&Bs accept children, and there is a strong case for making advance reservations. If you choose the serendipitous method, local tourist information centers are a good source for finding B&Bs as you go.

After narrowing down the choices, call or email the places where you might want to stay. If you are calling, keep time differences in mind and try to avoid the busy breakfast period or late in the evening. Most B&B owners are very helpful, and you can ask questions that guidebooks and websites might not cover. We find a tactful way to ask whether the B&B is really in the quiet countryside or if it is located just a few feet from a busy road. Impolite? Hey, it beats being surprised when you get there!

Note that B&B prices are sometimes quoted per person, not per room. Children generally do not stay for free; in fact, they often pay the same rate as adults.

Despite good research, there are no guarantees about what a B&B or hotel will be like when you arrive. We have made reservations at places that sounded fantastic only to be disappointed. We have gone without reservations and found wonderful places on the fly.

Sleep well!

Food, Glorious Food

Food, glorious food! Hot sausage and mustard!
While we're in the mood—Cold jelly and custard! Peas,
pudding and saveloys! What next is the question?
Rich gentlemen have it, boys—In-di-gestion!
—*Oliver!*, lyrics by Lionel Bart

It's a fact of life for parents traveling with children: meals can be a real challenge, and the price of dining out in London can be terrifically expensive. The good news is that today's London has more dining choices than ever before. Many of those new choices are family food friendly.

Full English Breakfast

If you're lucky, breakfast is included with your hotel room. All B&Bs include breakfast—that's the reason for the second *B*—and many hotels do as well. Breakfasts come in two basic varieties: continental and full English. For kids who normally survive on cereal, the continental breakfast may suffice. Depending on the establishment, a continental breakfast may include some type of puffed-rice cereal, maybe corn flakes, and muesli—a European cereal favorite. If your children must have Choca-Kicko-Snappy Pops, or some other nutritious breakfast cereal, they may be out of luck. In some places, a continental breakfast is simply bread, jam, coffee, and tea.

The full English breakfast is a heavy tradition. Heavy on eggs (served fried unless you ask for them another way), heavy on bacon or sausage, heavy on toast and jam. And as a bonus, the full English breakfast often comes with broiled mushrooms and broiled tomatoes. Not that there is anything nutritionally wrong with mushrooms or tomatoes, but the first time they are served at breakfast, non-British parents should be prepared for strange looks or inappropriate comments from their children. Sometimes, the meal includes baked beans as a side dish. This is the point where many overseas visitors draw the line in the cultural sand. Here's our read on full English breakfasts:

> Day 1—"Boy, these eggs and ham are great. What's with these broiled tomatoes and mushrooms?"
>
> Day 2—"Wow, another big breakfast. Good thing we're doing so much walking."
>
> Day 3—"No thanks, I'll pass on the baked beans."
>
> Day 4—"I wonder how much cholesterol is in this?"
>
> Day 5 through the end of the trip—"I don't ever want to see a broiled tomato or mushroom again."

The Brown Bag Solution

One solution for feeding the family is to bring soft-sided insulated picnic bags and use them for lunch on the go. You can purchase picnic lunch items from the elaborate food sections in the basement of Marks and Spencer or Harrods Food Hall or at a corner grocery. If the weather is good, head for Hyde Park, Green Park, St. James's Park, Regent's Park . . . you get the idea.

Consider including a few items in your suitcase to bring along to the picnics:

- Swiss army knife
- Disposable moist hand wipes
- Lightweight, waterproof ground cloth
- Corkscrew (for Mom and Dad's wine)

At the end of the trip, the padded insulated picnic bags are great for packing breakable souvenirs to carry home on the plane. Because of airport security restrictions, knives and corkscrews with blades cannot go in carry-on luggage.

Ready to Eat

In the capital city of the country that invented the sandwich, lunches should be a snap, right? Almost every street in central London overflows with sandwich and coffee shops. Although these largely cater to businesspeople on lunch breaks, they also work well for families in search of a quick meal. Costa and Pret a Manger are chains with fresh, reasonably priced lunchtime fare. Most patrons carry out food, but there are tables for those who wish to stay and eat. One advantage to carryout ("takeaway") is that cold carryout food is exempt from the hefty value added tax.

Teatime

"At any rate I'll never go THERE again!" said Alice as she picked her way through the wood. "It's the stupidest tea-party I ever was at in all my life!"

—*Alice's Adventures in Wonderland*, by Lewis Carroll

For the uninitiated, tea is not just a drink in England; it is a quintessential dining and social experience. Tea comes in all varieties, costs, and degrees of formality. When traveling with children, parents have a choice: find a less formal spot to enjoy teatime if the kids can't sit still for an hour, or, if they're more patient, go all out and do afternoon tea.

Afternoon tea generally consists of tea (naturally), scones with jam and clotted cream, pastries or cake, and perhaps even delicate sandwiches. There is nothing low fat or low cholesterol about it. Will kids like it? Probably, and you can always order something else to drink if they won't go for hot tea.

Sometimes tea can be substantial enough to serve as a substitute for an early dinner. Start the day with a full English breakfast and eat a nutritious snack at lunchtime, followed up by tea late in the afternoon, and another snack before bed. This meal-snack-meal-snack routine is probably not recommended by nutritionists, but it has some advantages on a family trip to

London. Because finding kid-acceptable lunches and dinners can be problematic, substituting tea for dinner avoids the issue of where to eat an evening meal with children. Also, meal-snack-meal-snack fits well into a busy day of sightseeing because it provides several breaks when a family can sit down and revive before heading back to the tourist routes.

Teatime formality notwithstanding, the staff at the restaurants in London's Fortnum & Mason department store seem to enjoy serving families. Well, maybe they just tolerate kids, but that's close enough. One afternoon, our children were restless after an hour of tea, scones, and cake. Dad and kids got up from the table to wander the store in search of toys. Meanwhile, the waitress implored Mom to stay and "relax away from the children . . . have another cuppa' and eat some more tarts!"

Many London hotels offer afternoon tea. Some—like the upscale Ritz, Four Seasons, and Brown's—are famous for over-the-top tea extravaganzas. But the average Londoner hardly has the time or the inclination for this level of daily tea ritual.

Room service at the Ritz—expensive, but kid-friendly

Pub Grub

So far we've covered breakfast, lunch, and tea. What about dinner? Some travel experts advise that pub food is a good bet because it is cheap and filling. To be blunt, some traditional pub food can sound unappetizing to children. However, today's pubs are as likely to serve cheeseburgers and ice cream as they are to offer bangers and spotted dick. You can probably find something on the menu that will please your children.

At the top of the pub food chain, the food (and prices) at "gastropubs" can be indistinguishable from that at a fine restaurant.

In London, much of the pub scene is generally geared not to families but to drinking beer and ale. In fact, some pubs do not admit children. How to tell whether a London pub is family friendly? Call ahead or check online. A few pubs have signs posted near the door, but many do not, requiring Mom or Dad to walk in, find a pub employee, and ask before bringing in the kids. Yes, this can be intimidating.

Outside London, pubs with family rooms are more common. The Four Alls pub in Welford-upon-Avon is one example of a family-oriented pub. Welford is a few miles upstream from its heavily touristed neighbor Stratford-upon-Avon. While staying at a nearby farmhouse B&B, we toured the Cotswolds by day, wandering back to Welford each evening. Whether it was for the decent food or the playground outside, the children kept suggesting that we return every night to the family room in "our" pub. Family rooms in some pubs may include pool tables and arcade games.

Other Choices

As a city with many immigrants, London boasts a sizable number of ethnic restaurants; good news if your kids like Asian, Indian, or Italian food. It is possible to find appetizing, reasonably priced meals in some of the city's ethnic establishments. It is also possible to find overpriced, uninspired food here.

With most children, you can't go wrong with plain pizza, but the trick in London is to find kid-friendly pizza. Cheese-and-tomato pizza sometimes features tomato slices instead of tomato sauce. This did not go over well with our young children, nor did the pizza with curry offered by a Pizza Hut in the Bayswater neighborhood. Pizza Express and Ask are popular London chains offering pizza and other Italian dishes. Celebrity chef Jamie Oliver oversees the Jamie's Italian chain of midscale restaurants with several London locations.

Food trucks and seasonal pop-up restaurants offer quick food options in many areas. Walking along the south bank of the Thames, what could be cooler than buying frozen yogurt from a converted double-decker London bus? Or lobster rolls and fish tacos from a refitted 1960s Volkswagen van? Or maybe a drink from a café housed in a vintage Airstream trailer (caravan).

Informal, cafeteria-style food is served at some London churches, museums, and historical sites. We've included many throughout the book. Here are a few examples:

- The Crypt Café at St. Martin-in-the-Fields (see the "Brass Rubbing" section)

- The café in the Victoria and Albert Museum (the first museum restaurant in the world)

- The cafeteria in the basement of Central Hall Westminster, right across the street from Westminster Abbey

- The Armouries cafeteria on the grounds of the Tower of London

Wagamama, the ubiquitous noodle chain, offers inexpensive and fresh Asian-inspired noodle dishes in locations throughout London. Wagamamas are usually clean, quick, and spartan; for kids who enjoy noodle-based soups and other dishes, this is a good choice. Coffee shops are everywhere in central London; Starbucks, yes, but others too, like Caffé Nero, Costa Coffee, and local outlets trying to survive in a corporate coffee culture.

Be aware that some mid- to upscale London restaurants do not open for dinner until 7:00 or 7:30 p.m. Fortunately, a number of moderately priced chain restaurants that serve dinner earlier have opened around London. In this case, the term *chain restaurant* does not mean fast-food places like McDonald's or Burger King, although you'll find these in London, too. We're referring to real sit-down restaurants like Bella Italia, Giraffe, Café Rouge, Carluccio's, and Jamie's Italian, to name a few. These places are informal and reasonable (by London standards), and—best of all—you don't have to wait until 7:30 p.m. to feed the family. Our visit to Bella Italia just off Oxford Street featured a family-pleasing menu served by friendly staff. To make the meal even more of a bargain, check websites for restaurant discounts.

Want to take the family out for a special meal? London has hundreds of moderate to expensive restaurants; many are independent and some are upscale restaurant chains. Keep in mind that restaurant meals in London are often much more expensive than in smaller cities.

Special Treats

A visit to London may broaden your children's food horizons. After discovering Nutella in London, our son craved Nutella sandwiches. For those who've never tasted it, Nutella is an Italian chocolate hazelnut spread, sort of a peanut butter for chocoholics. Our son fell in love with Cadbury chocolate bars, claiming that they were the best he had ever tasted. His notes on the subject follow, and we defer to him as an expert:

- Dairy Milk chocolate bars are the best . . . watch out for bars with nuts and raisins.

- Convince your parents to buy lots of Cadbury bars at the tax-free shops in the airport before you come home. After all, they need to use up all that leftover British money before the plane takes off.

- The Cadbury bars sold in the United States don't taste as good as the ones in the United Kingdom.

Our daughter had a more adventurous palate. On her first trip to London, she developed an affinity for scones topped with jam and clotted cream. On another trip she started drinking hot tea. Given that one can survive on English breakfasts and afternoon tea, this development ended the food crisis from her perspective.

Fish and chips is a traditional favorite that goes over well with many children. London "chippies" offer a variety of fish; a mild white fish like cod may be the best choice for kids. The fish is fried, as are the chips, of course, but visitors tend to burn a lot of calories walking around London.

Food truck—or food bus—along the Thames

PART FIVE

Did You Forget Anything?

Passport? Check! Suitcase? Check!
Cut-Off Shorts?
Camera? Check! Travel Journal? Check!
Guardians of the Past
Getting There
Getting around Town
Phones and the Internet
Medical and Money Matters
Britspeak
Time to Leave

Passport? Check! Suitcase? Check! Cut-Off Shorts?

Passports

Most foreign visitors need a valid passport to enter Britain. Visitors from the European Economic Area can enter the United Kingdom with a valid passport or national identity card. US, Commonwealth, and European Union citizens do not need a visa. Passports are required for the whole family, and children of all ages must have their own passports. In the United States, eligible individuals can apply for a passport online. You can also apply at a local passport acceptance site, including many post offices. In addition to a completed application form, adult US citizens need the following items to obtain a passport:

- Proof of age and citizenship
- Photo ID, such as a driver's license or government ID card
- A passport-quality photograph
- Money—passport fees are hefty, but an adult passport is valid for ten years
- Patience

We mention the last item because it routinely takes four to six weeks to get a passport, although you can opt for expedited service. Need a passport in a hurry? Apply at a regional US passport agency.

As we noted, children must have a passport to travel internationally. The application process for children under age sixteen who are US citizens generally requires the participation of both parents, and the application must be made in person at a passport agency or acceptance site. Parents must prove their identities, document their relationship to the child (birth, adoption, or guardianship court order), and provide consent for the passport to be issued. Children ages sixteen and seventeen follow a slightly different process.

Even with a valid passport, there are strict requirements for international travel by children when they are not accompanied by both parents. The protections are in place to guard against incidents in which one parent flees the country with a child in a custody dispute. Travel restrictions can come as a surprise when custody is not at issue or when one parent (or a grandparent) tries to take a child on an overseas trip. Generally, a notarized letter with specific consent for travel, signed by both parents, is advisable.

For more information on the US passport process, including updates on new passport features and requirements, check the State Department's website at http://travel.state.gov. For information on Canadian passports, see the Passport Canada website at www.ppt.gc.ca.

Luggage

From the carpet-bag she took out seven flannel night-gowns, four cotton ones, a pair of boots, a set of dominoes, two bathing-caps and a postcard album. Last of all came a folding camp-bedstead with blankets and eider-down complete, and this she set down between John's cot and Barbara's.
—*Mary Poppins*, by P. L. Travers

Advice on packing is de rigueur for most self-respecting travel guidebooks. Guess that means we have to include a section on the subject, but let's preface it with a confession: we enjoy planning and taking trips, but we dislike packing and transporting luggage. Short trips of a week or less are not too bad, but packing two or three weeks' worth of clothing and accessories for a family trip is a challenge.

Because the weather in London can vary so greatly, there is no ideal way to pack for a trip to London. Even for the summer months, we suggest planning a layered wardrobe: short-sleeved shirts, over which you can put a sweater and add a water-repellent jacket with a hood or hat. Dark colors don't show much dirt and, with a little luck, children can wear a pair of dark jeans for more than one day. If possible, pack clothes in colors and styles that can be mixed and matched easily.

It is virtually impossible to carry enough clean clothes for more than a week, especially when traveling with kids. On longer trips, this means doing laundry. (Arrgh!) Hotel laundry services are very expensive, but you can find launderettes in some central London neighborhoods. Spending time doing laundry is not our idea of vacation fun. We've done it on long trips, but it does seem like a waste of valuable touring time. Because children often manage to get spots and stains on otherwise clean clothes, pack some disposable stain removal wipes for quick cleanups. Also, take along some large plastic bags to store shoes and dirty clothes.

The more you pack, the heavier the luggage becomes, and not every child can lift a heavy suitcase. We suggest using relatively inexpensive, but sturdy, wheeled suitcases with good wide rollers and telescoping handles. Test luggage before buying it because some suitcases tip over easily, and tippy luggage is no fun when you are running to catch a train or an elevator.

There are times on a trip when you will have to lift the suitcases, so make sure that you can manage your bags. While some children may not be able to pick up a big suitcase, most kids are adept at carrying a heavy backpack to school every day. So consider backpacks or daypacks as part of the family luggage complement. Small backpacks work well as airplane carry-ons and can be used for picnics and hiking excursions during the trip.

Airline baggage allowances and restrictions are a major consideration when packing for a trip. The allowances vary by cabin, with first and business class passengers permitted to check more luggage than coach-class passengers. Travelers should be aware that European measurements defining carry-on luggage sizes are different from (read that as "smaller than") North American carry-on measurements.

As every seasoned traveler knows, busy airports are full of look-alike bags. For an inexpensive solution, tie some bright-colored ribbon on your family's bags and backpacks.

If you want to lock your suitcases, use locks approved by the US Transportation Security Administration (TSA). These locks are also accepted by UK security screeners.

Raingear?

In case you haven't heard, it rains in London. A lot. Before a trip, consider purchasing waterproof fabric spray and coating everything: shoes, jackets and coats, hats, backpacks, the children. On second thought, don't waterproof the kids, but do spray just about everything else. This will come in handy if it rains. Plus, if you go to all this effort, it probably won't rain one drop.

Not that obsessive? Well, at least consider lightweight rain jackets for the family. Of course, if it rains you could buy those garish, cheap plastic ponchos from a souvenir vendor in London. But that brings us to the next tip . . .

Rain in Britain? Maybe . . .

Blending In

You may *be* a tourist in London, but you don't have to *look* like one. Londoners sport all varieties of fashion, but few of them dress like stereotypical tourists. Beyond dressing like a tourist, some visitors just act like tourists. Constantly taking photographs or studying maps while standing in the middle of a crowded sidewalk is a sure sign of a tourist.

To blend in, dress conservatively and tastefully, carry a small camera in a pocket or bag, buy a compact foldout map and study it before hitting the street. Dressing conservatively and tastefully does not necessarily mean dressing up. Casual clothes are usually fine in London, but dark slacks and decent shirts blend in better than sweat suits and T-shirts advertising your favorite brand of beer.

Cultural stereotypes are problematic, but one characteristic often associated with tourists is loudness. Visitors who want to blend in should take this into consideration. Failure to use correct local terminology is another faux pas. Asking for directions to "the bathroom" instead of using the British terms *loo* and *toilet* marks you as a sure tourist. On the other hand, don't go overboard and adopt a fake accent—Londoners will know you are not a native anyway.

Camera? Check!
Travel Journal? Check!

Cameras

Taking a digital camera? Be sure to have a large enough media card to hold lots of shots. The cards that come with many cameras are probably inadequate. Using your phone as a camera? Think twice before uploading gigabytes of photo data while roaming. See the "Phones and Internet" section for more on data roaming.

Before leaving on your trip, make sure your camera is working properly. Finding out that a camera is malfunctioning is an unwelcome surprise during or after a vacation.

Computers

Taking a portable computer on a trip is a mixed blessing. Many travelers want or need to keep in touch online during vacations. But for the traveler, laptops and other electronic devices can engender additional security screening at airports. Then there's the weight and bulk of packing and carrying even the smallest device, along with concerns about loss or theft. Quality London hotels usually offer in-room Wi-Fi, but they often charge exorbitant fees for getting online. Don't forget a plug adapter to connect to British electrical outlets.

Finding free Wi-Fi connections in central London isn't too difficult, although many are located in coffee shops, bars, or pubs, where you are expected to buy something for the privilege. Large swaths of the city are Wi-Fi hot zones, but not all of these are free. A few Internet cafés survive in London, where you can get online for a couple of pounds. This can be a cheaper option than paying hotel connection charges, although public computers (and clientele) can be a bit grubby at some locations.

Exercise care when using a non-British smartphone, tablet PC, or other wireless device in London. Mobile data roaming rates can be outrageous. Our advice? Make sure your device is unlocked and usable in the UK, then buy a British SIM card and a short-term data plan when you arrive in London. There are mobile stores in London airports and throughout the city. Buying a SIM card before you leave home, renting a device, buying a "world wide" data plan, or signing up for your home provider's overseas roaming plans all seem to cost more than just getting one in London.

Online in the British Library

Postcards, Scrapbooks, and Journals

As a family activity, mail yourselves a postcard from London. Buy a postcard showing a favorite London site and write a note to yourselves about what a wonderful trip you are having. Then find a mailbox—only an old-fashioned red postbox will do—and take a photograph of your children as they mail the postcard home. When you get back from vacation, the postcard and the photo will be great additions to a scrapbook.

A trip to London gives kids ample opportunity to collect things: ticket stubs from trains, theaters, museums, and brochures from hotels, airplanes, and tourist information counters. Consider relaxing your parental tendency to throw away all this junk. Let the children collect items as a record of the trip. Intersperse this collected material with photographs, and you'll have the makings of a memorable family keepsake.

Another way to record the trip is to take along travel journals for every family member. Of course you can do this online if everyone's carrying their own device. Most school-age children can use the practice on their writing skills, and young artists may want to include drawings in their journals. At the end of each day on the trip, take a few minutes to write in the journals. After a busy day of touring, the children may have a hard time staying awake long enough to fill a page, but it is surprising how fast the details of a vacation can be forgotten, so a journal can be an important way to help preserve travel memories.

Sights and Sounds

Sightseeing is on every tourist's agenda, but to fully appreciate London be prepared to listen as you tour the city. Some examples:

- Be anywhere close to Big Ben at the top of the hour. Noon and midnight are best (twelve *BONGS*).

- Listen for accents. The trained ear will hear a variety of languages and accents, some typical of London natives, some not. Watch out or you're liable to start speaking with a local "twist" after a few days.

- Listen to the organist practice in Westminster Abbey or stop by a lunchtime concert at St. Martin-in-the-Fields church.

Children can listen for train whistles, church bells, station announcements in the Tube, overheard conversations of local children, shouted commands at the changing of the guards—all uniquely local and all a part of their trip memories.

Guardians of the Past

Overseas visitors to Britain may notice that many historic landmarks are owned or operated by one of two organizations: the National Trust or English Heritage. The Trust is a non-profit group that preserves historic land, gardens, and buildings in Britain. English Heritage is similar, except that it is government backed. Each organization operates a different set of properties, but there is some overlap. At Stonehenge, for example, the National Trust owns the land, and English Heritage operates the site.

A visitor's pass from one of these organizations can save you fees on admission to historic sites; however, neither organization operates many of the major tourist attractions in London. Visitors who are not venturing out of the city may not save enough to justify purchasing a pass.

Families traveling to Britain need to evaluate the merits of purchasing passes based on their itineraries and the ages of their children. Most passes are sold in adult and child versions, but many of the historic sites offer reduced admission prices for children. On one trip, we discovered that purchasing passes for the two adults and paying cash for the children's admission tickets made the most economic sense.

Keep in mind that many major museums in London offer free admission, so don't buy a pass assuming that you will save money on museum tickets.

English Heritage Overseas Visitor Pass

This pass admits visitors into English Heritage sites only and is good for nine or sixteen days. English Heritage properties in London include the Chapter House in Westminster Abbey, the Jewel Tower near Parliament, Kenwood House, and the Wel-

lington Arch. Purchase the pass online at www.english-heritage
.org.uk or at many English Heritage–operated properties in
Britain. English Heritage also offers annual memberships that
include admission to sites.

National Trust and Royal Oak

The National Trust sells touring passes of different lengths
that provide entry into trust properties. Americans can join the
Royal Oak Foundation, an affiliate of the National Trust, and
get free admission to all Trust properties for a year. A family
Royal Oak membership is a relative bargain. Like English
Heritage, the National Trust operates only a few properties in
central London, but the Trust has partnerships with a number of
smaller central London museums such as the Benjamin Franklin
House, that offer 50 percent discounts on admission for Trust
and Royal Oak members. Information on properties, passes,
and memberships can be found on the National Trust website at
www.nationaltrust.org.uk and the Royal Oak website at
www.royal-oak.org.

Historic Royal Palaces Pass

Historic Royal Palaces is the governmental agency that administers Hampton Court Palace, Kensington Palace, the Banqueting House, the Tower of London, Kew Palace, and Queen Charlotte's Cottage. The agency sells passes that admit visitors to several palaces at a savings over individual admission charges. Purchase passes and individual tickets online at www.hrp.org.uk. Historic Royal Palaces offers annual memberships including memberships in its American Friends affiliate.

London Pass

The London Pass is a commercial pass that provides admission to many tourist attractions in London. The London Pass is not cheap, so review the list of attractions covered before purchasing one of these cards to make certain that you will get your money's worth. In general, to make the card worthwhile, you need to visit a fair number of sites (that charge admission fees) during a relatively short time period. One huge benefit of the London Pass is that pass holders usually get to bypass regular ticket lines. During peak months, that alone may be reason enough to invest in a pass. The London Pass website is www.londonpass.com.

Getting There

European visitors to London have the luxury of choice: they can fly, take a train through the Chunnel (English Channel tunnel), or come by ferryboat. Almost everyone else faces a long plane ride; for families traveling with young children, this journey can be a challenge. The trick is keeping the challenge from becoming an ordeal.

Look! It's a Bird; It's an Eight-Hour Plane Ride

Many airlines offer overnight flights to London, leaving the North American East Coast in the evening and arriving somewhere between 7:00 a.m. and 10:00 a.m. London time the next day. Although it does mean one less night in a hotel, the overnight trip is a drag on the whole family. A few East Coast flights leave in the morning and arrive in London the same evening (local time). An advantage of this schedule is that it avoids an overnight flight and may reduce the effects of jet lag. Return flights are somewhat easier because they usually leave London in the early afternoon and, flying with the sun, arrive in North America in the late afternoon or around dinnertime. Either way, it is a long ride.

West Coast travelers face nearly ten hours in the air on a non-stop flight to London. Flights leaving Los Angeles at 6:00 p.m. arrive in London around noon the next day. This is a long flight, and some families may prefer to break it up with an overnight stop along the way.

This section examines survival tips for families on the flight segment from the North American East Coast to London. These tips can be adjusted for longer flights or travel to London from other countries.

If you leave on an evening flight, consider eating dinner before boarding. Once airborne, decline the meal on the plane.

This action may earn some funny looks from the flight attendants, but if you eat dinner on the plane at 8:00 or 9:00 p.m. Eastern Time, you'll be offered breakfast four hours later as the plane approaches the United Kingdom. This out-of-sync meal schedule can add to jet lag.

On the flight over, try to adjust to a London schedule as soon as possible. One strategy: set your watch to London time when you get on the plane. Wow, it's midnight already, time to go to sleep! Now convince your kids (and yourself) that the next seven hours on the plane are actually a normal night: you ate dinner at 6:00 p.m., got on the plane at 7:00 p.m., went to bed at 8:00 p.m., tried to sleep for five hours, woke up and had breakfast, then landed in London.

Okay, it's really 2:00 a.m. US Eastern Time when the plane arrives in London and you probably got no sleep, but you have to *believe* it was a normal night or risk falling asleep soon after landing in London. This schedule almost works, especially if it is a bright, sunny morning when you get off the plane (sunlight seems to reduce the impact of jet lag).

After landing in London, try to follow a normal schedule. You'll be tired, but don't take a nap (unless afternoon naps are still a part of your child's daily routine). If caffeine helps, grab some coffee or tea early in the day. Eat meals at regular London times and try to stay awake until at least 9:00 p.m. In theory, by the next day you will have made the switch to London time. Good luck with this routine, particularly if traveling with young children.

Flying long-distance business or first class can be a better experience than flying economy class. Upper-class seats usually convert to flat "beds," making it relatively easy to get a few hours of real sleep on the journey. First and business class passengers can even get showers, spa treatments, and breakfast at special arrivals lounges in London airports. *Ahhh . . .*

For families, the airplane trip to London can be trying, at best. We have outlined a possible schedule to ease the transition.

Here are some additional tips to make children more comfortable on the flight.

Motion Sickness and Ear Problems

If your child is prone to motion sickness, be prepared before getting on the plane. Check with a pediatrician about whether the child can safely take motion sickness medication. Drowsiness is one side effect of some medications. That's not a bad thing for sleeping on the plane, but dehydration is another possible side effect. Drinking lots of water can have unwanted side effects, especially considering the lines for lavatories on crowded airplanes.

Some children have success with pressure point wristbands (brand-name Sea-Band). These elastic bands apply gentle pressure to a point on the inside of each wrist. How and why they work are a mystery to us. Is it a scientific principle, or is it like the magic feather that convinced Dumbo the Elephant that he could fly? Regardless of how they work, wristbands are a drug-free alternative for preventing motion sickness. Another motion sickness suggestion is to feed children only small amounts of bland food before and during the flight. This may help prevent sickness.

Expecting motion sickness to be inevitable while flying with a child? Be prepared for the worst and pack a change of clothes in a zip-top plastic bag—in addition to clean clothes if the child vomits, the bag provides a place to stash the dirty garments. Consider dressing your child in an old sweat suit, and then throw it away in the airport if it gets messed up. Wasteful? Yes. But who wants to carry around a plastic bag with barfed-on clothes?

On an airplane, changes in air pressure can cause ear problems for children and adults alike. Parents can try giving children something to chew during takeoff and landing, and babies can suck the heck out of their pacifiers to equalize pressure. Some earplugs use ceramic filters to slowly equalize air pressure. The earplugs (brand-names EarPlanes and Flitemates) also block out some noise, so they have an added benefit when you are trying to sleep on the plane.

Seating Arrangements

Airplane seating has become a not-so-funny joke, as hundreds of passengers are crammed into narrow seats with almost no legroom. A family lucky enough to travel first or business class can sit back, relax, and try to enjoy the flight. Others should read on for some coping tips.

Adults can usually survive a restless airborne night, but young children often fall apart without adequate sleep. Adults traveling with children may want to get window seats for the kids, with an adult in the seat next to each child. This works well on planes with rows of two seats by the cabin wall: parent and child can travel side by side with no strangers sitting next to the child. When it is time to sleep, the kids can prop a pillow against the cabin wall or lean against Mom or Dad.

Seats just in front of a bulkhead are good because there will be no noisy people behind you when you are trying to sleep. Keep in mind that these seats may not recline as far as other seats (if they recline at all). Parents may prefer seats facing a bulkhead because this provides a sense of privacy. Some airlines offer special seats/cots for children under age two. These seats attach to a cabin bulkhead wall and allow the child to lie down or sit up. To arrange for this, check with the airline when making reservations.

Although some airlines allow an infant to be held in the lap of an adult, we question the safety of this practice and the sanity of anyone who plans to hold a baby for the duration of an overseas plane ride. The "lap baby" fare is cheap, but buying a separate seat for a baby allows parents to use an approved child safety seat or harness on board. Seats or harnesses should be approved for use on an airplane by the US Federal Aviation Administration (FAA) or the British Civil Aviation Authority. The CARES harness (www.kidsflysafe.com) is approved by the FAA.

Generally, seats over the wings near the center of the plane have a smoother ride than seating near the tail or the nose. Think of a plane as a seesaw—the least motion will be near the center pivot point rather than at the ends. Note to nervous flyers: don't think of an airplane as a seesaw; think of it as a puffy cloud gliding calmly through a bright-blue sky.

Some airlines have eliminated the practice of allowing passengers to preselect seating locations. Others do offer seat choices but tend to pile on extra fees. Members of an airline's frequent-flier program may find it easier to preselect seats. Regardless of the airline's stated policy, decide in advance where you want to sit. Try to let the airline know that you are traveling with children, and request the preferred seat assignment when purchasing tickets and again when checking in for the flight. Some airlines preassign seat locations for parents with infants at the time of booking and also assign parents and children to adjacent seats in advance. There may be fees for preferred seating of families.

At the gate, families with young children usually board first. Listen for the boarding announcement to take advantage of this privilege.

The Class System

Most families purchase coach/economy tickets out of economic necessity and suffer through the indignities of "cattle class." Those fortunate enough to fly business class or first class to London have a much different experience. The flight times are the same, although someone once pointed out that passengers in the front of the airplane arrive a fraction of a second ahead of coach passengers seated in the back. The business class experience from boarding to landing can be much less stressful, with faster check-in, larger baggage allowances, separate departure and arrival lounges, better food, and humanely sized

Ahhh . . . business class

seating. British Airways, Virgin Atlantic, and other airlines offer flat-bed business class service, where passengers might actually get some sleep on the way to London. Virgin Atlantic even calls this "upper class," as if we need reminding that the class system operates in the air.

Recognizing that not everyone can afford to fly business class, some airlines have added premium economy service. For a moderate increase in ticket price, this class includes more legroom and a slight upgrade in amenities and service. Premium economy can be a good compromise for traveling families who can afford the increased fares.

In-Flight Distractions (and Fluffy the Bear)

Sleep is the goal of veteran travelers on overnight flights. It is easier for adults to ignore in-flight distractions, but this may be more of a challenge for families. If sleep is impossible on the plane, parents face hours of entertaining restless children. Fortunately, on long overseas flights, some airlines provide activity kits for kids. These are good for an hour or so . . . then what? Listening to the audio channels or watching the in-flight movies and games? Some airline entertainment is pretty mild, but not everything is appropriate for children.

In 2014, British Airways surveyed several thousand family fliers about how to keep kids occupied on flights. Some recommendations:

- New toys and games entertain kids for longer than old ones.
- Wrap items like presents and hand them out at intervals.
- Focus on bringing activities, not static toys.
- Bring games that will keep kids occupied for more than a few minutes.

We suggest letting each child carry a small backpack filled with paperback books, small games or toys, a journal/sketchbook, markers and pens, and maybe a stuffed animal. Don't pack expensive items that may get lost on a long trip.

A special note about Fluffy the Bear (or whatever the name/ species of your child's favorite stuffy). If Fluffy absolutely must go on the trip, plan in advance how to keep track of him. Perhaps Fluffy needs his own identifying luggage tag. Maybe he really would like to "ride" in the suitcase or backpack and come out only at bedtime. Tracking down Fluffy if he gets left in an airport lounge, on the plane, in a taxi, on a train, or in a hotel is not how parents want to spend their travel time and emotional energy!

London's Airports

Most long-haul flights arrive at one of two London airports: Heathrow, about sixteen miles (twenty-six kilometers) west of central London, or Gatwick, twenty-eight miles (forty-five kilometers) south of downtown.

Generally, arriving at Gatwick is less complicated because that airport is smaller and not as busy as Heathrow. Getting to downtown London is easy because there is frequent express train service from the airport to Victoria rail station; the trip takes thirty to forty minutes. Nonexpress trains take a few minutes longer but cost less. Thanks to Gatwick's layout, which includes an elevated shuttle train between terminals, passengers can use luggage carts almost all the way from baggage pickup at the airport to the taxi stand at London's Victoria station. Victoria is convenient for hotels and attractions near Buckingham Palace and south of Hyde Park.

For visitors who are not headed for downtown London, or if Victoria rail station is not convenient, there are trains from the Gatwick rail station to London Bridge rail station and to

Heathrow Airport Terminal 5

other locations around London. Because London is nearly thirty miles away, taking a taxi from Gatwick to central London is an expensive and lengthy proposition.

Arriving at Heathrow? The size of this airport can be daunting, as are the transportation choices. Heathrow has its own high-speed rail link from the airport to Paddington station in downtown London; travel time is about fifteen minutes. Look for Heathrow Express signs in the arrivals area. A nonexpress train (Heathrow Connect) also follows this same route. Paddington station is convenient for hotels in Bayswater, Mayfair, and areas north of Hyde Park. Most passengers taking the train from Heathrow to Paddington will require a taxi to complete their journeys.

The London Underground (Tube) also serves Heathrow and provides the least expensive way to reach downtown. But visitors traveling with children (and/or with lots of luggage) might want to avoid the Tube at this point. Reasons? Little space for luggage, crowded during rush hours, transfers often required, and difficult-to-negotiate stairs in some stations.

The National Express company (www.nationalexpress.com) operates various bus/coach services from airports to central London and also connections between London's airports.

A taxi ride from Heathrow to downtown is possible, albeit expensive. An airport transfer service can be a logistically simple way to get between London and its airports. Reliable services meet visitors at the airport and take them directly to their hotels. Transfer services tend to be a bit less expensive than genuine London taxis, but they are less strictly regulated, so service levels and prices can vary. However, with London's heavy traffic, it is hard for any on-the-road transportation service to beat the express rail services.

WHERE? WHEN? £?

AIRPORTS

Heathrow Information
  Airport website: www.heathrowairport.com
  Heathrow Express: www.heathrowexpress.com
  Heathrow Connect: www.heathrowconnect.com
Gatwick Information
  Airport website: www.gatwickairport.com
  Gatwick Express: www.gatwickexpress.com

Green Travel

Underground, overground, wombling free,
The Wombles of Wimbledon Common are we.
Making good use of the things that we find,
Things that the everyday folks leave behind.

—"The Wombling Song," by Mike Batt

Airplanes contribute to global warming by spewing carbon dioxide and other pollutants into the atmosphere. Leisure travelers face an ethical dilemma when flying because their trips are by choice rather than of necessity. As awareness grows, some airlines are adopting carbon-neutral policies and including environmental fees in ticket prices. Other airlines offer fliers voluntary carbon-offset donation options as part of the ticketing process. One way that individuals can offset the impact of travel is to purchase carbon credits through an environmental organization like the Carbon Fund (www.carbonfund.org).

Getting around Town

Which is the way to London Town,
To see the King in his golden crown?
One foot up and one foot down,
That's the way to London Town.

Which is the way to London Town,
To see the Queen in her silken gown?
Left! Right! Left! Right! Up and down,
Soon you'll be in London Town!

Which is the way to London Town?
Over the hills, across the down,
Over the ridges and over the bridges,
That is the way to London Town.

And what shall I see in London Town?
Many a building old and brown.
Many a real, old-fashioned street
You'll be sure to see in London Town.
— Traditional children's rhyme

Finding Your Way

In reference to London, the term *street plan* is an oxymoron; there is no plan to London's streets. This city evolved from the streetscape laid down in Roman times. It was abandoned, burned, and rebuilt by Saxons, Normans, and Victorian reformers. It was flattened by Nazi bombs, rebuilt, and modernized. The result? Tourists need a good map and a fair sense of direction to avoid becoming hopelessly lost.

Even without a map or GPS, there are clues to finding your way in London. No, we don't mean relying on the position of the sun to determine east and west. We have tried this method, but it is useless at night or in London's often cloudy weather. Instead we suggest becoming familiar with London's postal codes. They have a certain logic to them. For example, *N* is north and *W* is west. The postal code gives an indication of a location relative to central London. Unfortunately, the numbers that make up the rest of the postal code are no help to the lost tourist, and they sometimes appear to have been assigned at random. If you are in zone W1, don't count on finding zone W2 around the corner.

Here are some key postal codes, with some of the areas they cover and interesting visitor sites in each postal code. For your sanity, we're showing only the first two or three letters/digits of the complete postal code:

- W1 (Mayfair, Marylebone): Royal Academy of Arts, shopping along Oxford, Regent, and Piccadilly streets
- W2 (Paddington, Bayswater): Hyde Park, Little Venice
- WC1 (Bloomsbury): British Museum
- WC2 (Strand, Covent Garden): London Transport Museum, National Gallery, Trafalgar Square
- W8 (Kensington): Kensington Palace
- SW7 (Knightsbridge, South Kensington): Victoria and Albert Museum, Science Museum, Natural History Museum
- SW1 (Westminster): Parliament, Westminster Abbey, Buckingham Palace, Victoria rail station, Churchill War Rooms
- EC3 (City of London, east): Tower of London
- EC4 (City of London): St. Paul's Cathedral
- E20 (formerly Walford, the fictitious borough in the BBC's *EastEnders* television show): Olympic Park
- NW1 (Regent's Park, Marylebone): London Zoo, Sherlock Holmes Museum, Regent's Park
- SE1 (Southwark): Globe Theatre, HMS *Belfast*, Imperial War Museum, Tower Bridge

When planning a trip to London, intrepid Internet explorers can use online mapping websites to help locate streets in the city. Simply enter a street name or postal code, and the mapping website provides color maps of the area at various levels of detail. Watch out for outdated maps, even on the Internet. When in London, most visitors will want a printed map of the city, balancing portability with level of detail. Tiny, foldable pocket maps are easy to carry and inconspicuous; printed maps with more details can be huge and ungainly. Smartphones or tablets with access to maps are the high-tech alternative.

If London seems large, that's because it is. Trivia fans and lost tourists will be interested to read that London is about 660 square miles, filled with more than eight million residents.

Underground and Bus

Paddington decided the Underground was quite the most exciting thing that had ever happened to him . . . "I shall always travel on this Underground in the future," said Paddington, politely. "I'm sure it's the nicest in all London."

—*A Bear Called Paddington*, by Michael Bond

Thank heavens for London's Underground (Tube) and bus systems, because driving in London is a tourist's worst nightmare. By all means, use the Tube and bus as your primary transport in the city.

The Underground system is augmented by commuter rail lines, notably the London Overground, which is fully integrated into the regional electronic fare card system. A new Crossrail system will connect eastern and western London suburbs. Central London Crossrail stations will integrate with the Underground and help speed east-west journeys in the city. Service begins in 2018.

Kids generally enjoy trips on both the Tube and London's red double-decker buses (riding on the top level, in the front seats, of course). A word of caution, however: avoid rush hours. The crush on the Tube is disconcerting for a six-foot-tall adult; it can be frightening for a four-foot-tall child. Bus travel during rush hour is maddeningly slow. Hours to avoid are generally weekdays 8:00 a.m. to 9:30 a.m. and 4:30 p.m. to 6:00 p.m.

The normal operating hours of the Tube are:

- Monday through Saturday from about 5:00 a.m. to just after midnight (1:00 a.m. on some lines and stations)
- Sunday 7:00 a.m. to midnight or slightly later

However, some lines are starting to operate overnight as Transport for London rolls out extended weekend hours.

Transport for London divides the city into travel zones; most of the central London tourist attractions are in Zone 1. The zone numbers get higher farther afield. For example, suburban Kew Gardens is in Zone 4. Visitors will want to choose a ticket option based on when they will travel, where they intend to go, and how long they are staying in London.

Transport for London offers a confusing array of tickets and fares. There are individual trip tickets, single and multiday Travelcards, and electronic Oyster cards. Cash purchase of single tickets is the most expensive option.

Paper Travelcards—good on buses, the Underground/Tube, local trains, and the Docklands Light Railway—make sense for some visitors, who can purchase one-day peak or off-peak Travelcards, or seven-day Travelcards. (Peak means travel before 9:30 a.m. on weekdays.) Child Travelcards are available. Travelcards can be purchased online and mailed in advance of a trip. You can also buy Travelcards at Tube stations in London, and you will receive an Oyster card that has been programmed to work like a Travelcard. Try to match the number of days on the Travelcard to the length of your visit; decide if you'll actually use the card on the days of arrival and departure.

Fares for Oyster card users are generally the lowest; there is a daily price cap on the cards, no matter how far or often you travel. Technically, it's more complicated than that, but the price cap is worthwhile. Oyster cards can be purchased online or in London from Tube stations and other locations including

Heathrow airport. Users pay a deposit for the card, then load it with money, choosing from a variety of options. Transport for London is pioneering contactless credit and debit card technology for bus and Underground fares. (Contactless cards have radio frequency chips that allow users to purchase without stopping at a cash register, entering a PIN, etc.) Generally, credit/debit cards issued in the United Kingdom work on this system; cards issued elsewhere may work, but be wary of overseas transaction fees that may accrue. See the "Money Matters" section for more information.

Symbols of London

Transport for London's fare options get even more confusing for families who want to take advantage of reduced fares for children. Children ages eleven to fifteen travel for very low cost, but may need a photo identification card issued by Transport for London. This is hardly practical for most overseas visitors, so buy a child rate Travelcard instead. People sixteen and older pay adult fares unless they are London residents with photo IDs.

So what's the best deal? Bargain hunters can check the Transport for London website at www.tfl.gov.uk if they are prepared to do some research. Visitors who just want convenience and unlimited travel can purchase the appropriate Travelcard and/or Oyster card before going through a turnstile.

Are the buses and subways safe? Most of the system usually feels safe. Pickpockets and beggars can be a problem in some Tube stations, and larger security threats are taken very seriously. Based on personal experience, evacuating a rail station because of a bomb threat is no laughing matter. Those are rare exceptions, however, and the Tube is generally a safe, dependable way to get around London. Here are some tips for safe Tube travel:

- Get a good map and plan Tube journeys before departure (Google Maps and other apps include detailed public transportation routes for London). Don't wander around the subway station looking like a lost tourist and an easy mark.

- Use a travel wallet to keep money out of sight. Sure, it's awkward to dig under your shirt or jacket every time you need cash, but a travel wallet will foil pickpockets.

- Don't leave bags or packages sitting unattended. Transport police may suspect a bomb and blow up your bag of souvenirs.

- Have one adult quickly distribute tickets/passes to family members just before boarding a bus or going through the Tube ticket turnstiles. Then collect the tickets and put them in a safe place.

- Touch Oyster cards to the yellow readers in the starting station and when leaving the destination station.

- Hold children's hands.

- Mind the gap! Everyone's favorite Transport for London phrase, this refers to the gap between the train and the platform at some Tube stops.

- Look for electronic signs on platforms that tell how long until the next train arrives and where it is heading. The signs display the final stop of the next train.

- Changing between different Underground lines in a station can often involve a very long walk through connecting passageways or across streets. Because of all the passageways, stairs, and escalators in Underground stations, it is sometimes quicker to walk short distances on London streets rather than take a short ride on the Tube.

The advantage of bus travel is that riders can sightsee while journeying around London. There are a huge number of bus routes in central London, and the maps and route/schedule information posted at each bus stop can be confusing, however. Use a transportation app or consult the online journey planner on the Transport for London website. You cannot simply hop on a London bus and buy a ticket—you must have an Oyster card, Day Travelcard, or contactless payment card.

Keep in mind that buses generally stop only at marked stops. There are automatic stops and "request" stops, where you must hail a bus to get on or indicate that you want to get off. Special night bus routes operate overnight and provide public transportation when the Tube is closed and taxis are scarce.

Taxi!

The driver looked hard at Paddington and then at the inside of his nice, clean taxi. "Bears is sixpence extra," he said, gruffly.

—*A Bear Called Paddington*, by Michael Bond

The black London taxi is as much a symbol of the city as is Tower Bridge or Big Ben. In recent years, the traditional black paint has been replaced by garish advertising painted on the cabs. We suspect that most parents waiting in the taxi queue hope to get into a traditional black taxicab, while their kids are rooting for the cab painted in retro-psychedelic colors.

No matter what the color, a real London taxi is a reliable, if expensive, way to get around town. Unlike some cities, where almost anyone with a driver's license can operate a cab, London requires taxi drivers to acquire a detailed understanding of London's streets and sites. London taxi drivers know where you're going.

After a long plane journey, an overseas visitor's first impression of London might be the inside of a taxi. Jet-lagged kids wake up fast when they ride in the taxi's rear-facing jump seats, hang on for dear life, and realize they're ON THE WRONG SIDE OF THE ROAD!

London has other taxilike conveyances. Order a taxi from a hotel, and you may get a private car service or minicab. Be aware that the training of the driver and the condition of the vehicle can vary by car company. Minicabs cannot pick up passengers on the street; you have to telephone a minicab company to arrange a ride. Riders can also use smartphone apps to summon ride-sharing services in London.

A word about costs. London's official taxicabs use a metering system that records time and distance traveled. Minicabs are allowed to charge what they like; some use meters, but most have set fees. So the laws of economics apply, one of which is "It's easy to take money from tourists." In a taxicab, be wary of the few drivers who will deliberately take longer-than-necessary routes, sometimes with an excuse of avoiding traffic jams or roadwork. In a taxi or minicab, get an estimate of the fare before starting a journey. If traveling with lots of luggage, make sure the taxi can carry it all. Official London taxis can carry five people, a couple of big suitcases in the passenger compartment, and a bag or two next to the driver. A limited number of official London taxis are Metrocabs, which can carry six passengers. Minicabs and shared ride vehicles may have different passenger capacities and space for baggage.

Finally, one other potential hazard is the so-called taxi tout. Working airports and rail stations, these guys pounce on tourists, carry bags to a car outside, and promise low fares. Two problems: the fares are usually not low and the practice of touting is illegal.

A London cab

Phones and the Internet

It wasn't often that Paddington made a telephone call—for one thing he always found it a bit difficult with paws.
—*Paddington Goes to Town*, by Michael Bond

Communication has come a long way since the days of the traditional red London telephone booth. Today, people are much more likely to communicate using mobile phones or computers. The iconic phone booths still make a great photo op, however.

Phone Number Formats

Telephone listings in local London publications don't always follow a consistent format, so we've standardized most of the telephone numbers listed in this book. London phone numbers are eleven digits long, most begin with the London area code (020), and they look like this:

020 #### ####

But you don't always use all eleven digits:

- From outside the United Kingdom, start with the 011 international access code, followed by 44 (the UK country code), then 20 (dropping the first zero of the London area code), and the eight-digit phone number.

- Within greater London, drop the 020 city code and just use the eight-digit phone number.

- From elsewhere in the UK, use all eleven digits.

Outside London and/or for certain toll-free or national rate numbers, the eleven digits are split up a bit differently. All have a leading zero, then a geographical code that's between two and five digits, followed by the rest of the number. Strangely enough, a phone number does not always have eleven digits in less populated areas; consistency is not part of the vernacular in British telephone listings. We have seen phone numbers listed like this:

> 0207-123 4567
> (0) 207 123 4567
> (020) 7123 4567
> (0) 20 7123 4567
> (440) 20-7123 4567

Prepare to be confused!

Other Important Numbers

- Call 999 or 112 for emergency fire, police, and ambulance services.

- Call 101 (where available) for nonemergency public safety services.

- Call 100 for operator assistance.

- Directory assistance numbers vary by telephone company, but all begin with 118.

- Cell/mobile phones start with 07, followed by nine digits.

- Toll-free numbers start with 0800 or 0808 and generally cannot be reached from outside the UK.

- Other numbers starting with 08 have special rates. Usually these are less expensive when dialed from a landline, but cost more when called from mobile phones. The 08 freephone numbers sometimes cannot be called from outside the UK.

- Numbers starting with 09 are for premium calls—some of which we can't discuss in a family travel guidebook.

Calling Britain

To call Britain from the United States or Canada:

- Use the international access code (011).
- Then add the UK country code (44).
- Do *not* use the zero prefix on the British telephone number.
- Then add the rest of the phone number (for example: 20 7123 4567).

To call Britain from a European country:

- Use the international access code (00).
- Then add the UK country code (44).
- Do *not* use the zero prefix on the British telephone number.
- Then add the rest of the phone number (for example: 20 7123 4567).

London calling

Phoning Home

To call the United States or Canada from Britain:

- Use the international access code (00).
- Then add the US/Canada country code (1).
- Then add the area code and phone number (for example: 555 992-1234).

Most hotels add an outrageous surcharge to outgoing calls. Your long-distance carrier at home may have a toll-free access number that you can dial directly from overseas, which allows you to use a calling card and pay lower rates for international calls. There are a number of other free or low-cost ways to phone home: prepaid calling cards; international "call back" systems; web telephone services such as Skype; and Google Hangouts or an instant messaging service or app.

Pay Phones

Pay phones are a dying breed. Those that survive in London come in several varieties. While there are still coin-operated pay phones in a few places, most pay phones take only credit cards or phone cards. The prepaid phone cards can be purchased from shops all over the city. Authorities fight a losing battle with escort services and others who post pornographic advertisements in central London phone booths. Use caution before letting young children enter a phone booth.

Mobile Phones

A cell phone (called a "mobile" in Britain) is the communications device of choice for a huge number of London residents. For a visitor, however, taking a cell phone to a foreign country and using it there requires a bit of planning. Not all North American cell phones will operate in Britain without adjustments to hardware and/or service agreements. European cell phones operate on the same frequencies as those in Britain, but some North American cell phones do not. The cell phone industry changes constantly, and today's best advice is outdated almost as soon as it is written. But in general, here are some options for cell phone service.

Roam from home. Some cell phone providers offer worldwide (or country-specific) roaming for existing phones. Users can activate this service to coincide with an overseas trip, although there may be a minimum service period of a month or longer. This is rarely the lowest-cost option.

Rent a phone. Travelers can rent an international cell phone and take it on a trip. Companies that rent phones express-deliver them before you depart. Upon return, ship the phone back to the rental company. This arrangement works, although it entails the hassle and cost of receiving and returning the phone. And the cost of renting and calling can be a bit pricey.

Buy a cheap phone. Cell phone equipment has become so cheap that buying an international phone can be as economical as renting. A number of companies specialize in the sale of international cell phones, usually also providing airtime and a billing service. Like rentals, these phones are delivered before a trip, but the phone is yours to keep and perhaps use on a subsequent visit.

Add a SIM card. Here's a cost-effective option. Before traveling, buy a used or inexpensive cell phone that is capable of operating in the United Kingdom. After arriving in London, purchase a SIM card from a local communications store. SIM cards can be purchased with varying minutes of usage preloaded. The downside to purchasing a SIM card after arrival is that you won't know your cell phone number before the trip begins.

Unlock and go. It's possible that your cell phone will work with a British SIM card. Before you travel, the phone may need to be "unlocked" to break the stranglehold of the original cell phone company. With an unlocked phone, the user can buy a SIM card and limited-service plan after arriving in the UK.

Buy British. You can buy a phone and service package from one of many mobile phone companies in the United Kingdom.

Mobile phone stores sprout like mushrooms at airports and in London shopping areas. There are some great deals for those willing to shop around.

Voice over Internet

Taking a laptop, tablet, or smartphone on your trip? Use it to phone home. Services like Skype and Google Hangouts allow computer users to call over the Internet, both to other computers and to regular telephones. Calls between computers are often free. Most instant messaging apps offer video and voice capabilities as well.

If your device has only Wi-Fi capabilities, then you can call home only when you are connected to the Internet by Wi-Fi. But many devices have both Wi-Fi and cellular capabilities and can connect to British mobile data networks just like smartphones.

Apple store in Covent Garden

And like with a smartphone, you'll want to replace the device's SIM card with a British SIM card and purchase a short-term data plan once you arrive in London.

Communications devices and software change at lightspeed so check out what's new before your trip.

Website

By the way, the *Let's Take the Kids to London* website is

www.KidsToLondon.com

Check it out—we frequently update it with new information. You can also find us on Facebook, Twitter, and other social media sites.

Medical and Money Matters

Most people would rather not think about getting sick while on a long-planned vacation to London. Questions about money can also induce travel angst. In both cases, a little preparedness goes a long way.

Is There a Doctor in the House?

Many insurers will reimburse for emergency medical expenses abroad, but they may require travelers to contact them for authorization. Managed care plans can be sticklers about notification. A US or Canadian medical insurance card is probably useless in Britain, but take it anyway, especially if it includes the phone numbers to call to notify the insurer of a medical emergency. Notice that we said many insurers will *reimburse* emergency medical expenses. This means you may have to pay doctor, pharmacy, or hospital bills directly in Britain.

Before leaving home, check with your health insurance company to find out exactly what coverage your family will have while traveling abroad. If this information is not already available in medical plan documents you have on hand, get it in writing from the insurer.

The United Kingdom operates a national health insurance plan; anyone, even a tourist, can obtain emergency medical treatment through this plan. For visitors who are not European Union residents, anything more than emergency treatment is provided on a fee-for-service basis. Visitors from the European Union can use the European Health Insurance Card to obtain medical treatment in the UK, with some limitations.

If this medical insurance situation makes you uneasy, or if you do not have adequate medical insurance, then consider purchasing travelers' health insurance through a reputable travel agency or insurance company. Many plans are available, some of which can be combined with coverage for lost baggage, travel delays, and other vacation disasters.

What to do if you have a non-life-threatening medical problem in London? Maybe a child comes down with an ear infection. Here are some sources of medical help for visitors:

- Private walk-in medical clinics cater to tourists. For example, MediCentres are located in Victoria, Paddington, and Waterloo rail stations and other central London locations.

- Call the front desk of your hotel. Most large hotels have on-call physicians or arrangements with medical centers, but this service can be expensive.

- The National Health Service operates walk-in centers, minor injury units, and hospital accident/emergency departments.

- In an emergency, telephone 999 for ambulance services.

One tactic used by traveling families is to pack a fairly extensive medical kit for overseas travel. Sometimes just carrying this kit acts like a talisman to keep illness at bay. If someone in the family has a history of illness, be sure to check with a physician before traveling to determine appropriate medicines to take on the trip. Have the generic names of any prescription medicines, because brand names may be different outside your home country. In Britain, prescriptions are filled by chemists.

Money Matters (Boy, Does It!)

For inside his hat was not just one, but a whole pile of coins. There were so many, in fact, that the latest addition—whatever it had been—was lost for all time amongst a vast assortment of pennies, three penny pieces, sixpences; coins of so many different shapes, sizes and values that Paddington soon gave up trying to count them all.

—*Paddington Goes to Town*, by Michael Bond

You've probably concluded by now that a trip to London is going to cost a bundle. How big a bundle is something over which you have some control, but a family traveling to London needs a fair amount of money in British currency/cash, credit cards, ATM cards, or a combination of these.

The basic unit of currency in Britain is the pound sterling. A pound (£) is divided into 100 pence (p). Here are common British currency denominations:

- Bills—£5, £10, £20, £50

- Coins—1 pence, 2 pence, 5 pence, 10 pence, 20 pence, 50 pence, £1, £2

For many years, Britain operated a complex, nondecimal system of currency. Although that old system is gone, a tourist can still get confused, because the pound is also referred to as *sterling*, and, more colloquially, a pound is a *quid* or even a *bob*.

Fumbling with unfamiliar bills and coins can ruin your image as a savvy tourist, so become familiar with the look and feel of pounds and pence before you start spending them. Learning about British coins can be an educational game, so try to obtain some coins before the trip and let children play with them.

For a tourist, foreign currency looks so different that sometimes spending it hardly seems real. We call this the Monopoly

How much?

money syndrome. Maybe this is a good thing, because overseas travel can be so expensive that, for some people, just thinking about the cost can almost ruin the trip. But to avoid bankruptcy, learn the currency and make a mental conversion to your home currency when spending pounds.

Whack-a-Mole Currency Rip-Offs

If there is one lesson to be learned about money and overseas travel, it is this: many banks, credit card companies, debit card issuers, and airport money exchanges are out to rip you off. They do this by imposing fees—sometimes deliberately hidden fees—on foreign currency transactions. Here are a few lies and half-truths that banks and others try to foist on travelers heading abroad:

- If a local bank says: "We can get British pounds for you, in any amount, for just a small fee," it's forgetting to tell you: "But our exchange rate is about six percent worse than what you can get from an ATM once you arrive in the United Kingdom."

- If a credit card company says: "The card is good at thousands of places in the UK," it's forgetting to add: "For a fee of four percent on each purchase."

- If a bank says: "Sure your VISA debit card is good at ATMs in London," it's leaving out: "At the currency exchange rates set by VISA."

- And if your otherwise trustworthy local travel agency offers to sell you a convenient "tip pack" in British pounds, watch out; the markup can be outrageous.

Dynamic Currency Conversion

But wait, there's more. Let's say you use a credit card to rent a car at the airport. The rental company may offer to charge your card directly in your home country's currency instead of in pounds, "for your convenience." Or sometimes they don't offer a choice and automatically process the transaction in your home currency. This is *dynamic currency conversion*.

That may seem like a good deal, but when the car rental company charged your card in your home currency, it added a currency conversion fee as part of the transaction. Worse, because the transaction is considered foreign, your credit card company may add its own fee to the transaction. Bottom line: decline the offer and have the transaction processed in British pounds.

With all these potential traps, what can a traveler do? Read on for some hints, but keep in mind that today's best advice could easily change as new fees are imposed.

ATMs

Most people routinely use automatic teller machines to get cash at home, and there is no reason to stop using ATMs when traveling to London. ATMs are also known as *cash points* in Britain. Before traveling, check with your bank to make sure that your ATM card and personal identification number (PIN) will work overseas. Many foreign ATMs allow access to a checking account only, so don't count on being able to transfer funds between savings and checking through an overseas ATM.

Convenience is a good reason to use ATMs, but there's another bonus: ATMs usually offer the best currency exchange rates. Be sure to use fee-free ATMs in London. Normally, ATMs associated with major British banks do not charge a user fee, but machines in pubs, convenience stores, and other areas may impose a fee or offer poor exchange rates. At the airport, be leery of ATMs operated by currency exchange companies and even some that seem to be bank affiliated. They sometimes do not offer the best exchange rates. Look for the exchange rate on the ATM screen before finalizing your transaction.

Your own bank may charge a small fee for each ATM transaction in London. In this case, it is wise to make fewer, larger transactions, rather than to repeatedly hit up ATMs for £20 at a time. Some non-British banks have affiliations with British banks that allow customers fee-free ATM use, but be careful: some banks charge a percentage fee for overseas ATM use. One last caution: even bank ATMs have started adding optional dynamic currency conversion. If the ATM offers to process the cash withdrawal in your home currency, decline this option.

Credit Cards

Plastic is just as fantastic in London as it is at home. VISA and MasterCard are widely accepted in the UK, and credit card transactions are generally converted from pounds to your local currency at favorable exchange rates.

VISA and MasterCard International corporations add a small percentage fee for all foreign transactions. There is no escaping this fee. But the credit card issuer—the bank or credit union that issued the card—can also add another, larger overseas transaction fee. Check with your bank and, if it has this fee, find another credit card that does not. Possibilities in the US include certain cards issued by Capital One, USAA Savings Bank, British Airways, and some credit unions.

We warned earlier about dynamic currency conversion. To avoid this, refuse to sign any credit card receipt that is not charged in the local currency. Just hand it back and say "Charge it in pounds." Some merchants may plead ignorance or claim that their credit card systems automatically charge the purchase in your home currency. That's not cricket, so play hardball here. The merchants' agreements with credit card companies require them to offer the choice of paying in local currency. In a pinch, sign the receipt and write on it "Merchant refused to charge in local currency." Then dispute the dynamic currency conversion charge through the credit card company.

Chip and pin. In Britain, credit card users insert their cards into the front of a card reader and then enter a personal identification number into the card reader's keypad. This is the chip-and-pin system. Many US credit cards are magnetic swipe cards that require a signature. If you don't have a chip-and-pin card, you might encounter some problems using credit cards in London, especially at unmanned locations like gasoline pumps and train station ticket machines. Check with your credit card company before you depart to see if it issues chip-and-pin cards; if you cannot obtain one, look for booths with people in them when using your credit card.

Don't leave home without it. Before leaving home, contact the customer service department of your credit card companies and bank ATM card issuers and inform them that you will be traveling overseas. The reason? Credit card companies and banks watch transactions accumulating on cards. If these go from Wal-Mart $13.99, the Gap $29.95 . . . to Harrods £24.01, Fortnum & Mason £50.49, it may look like someone has stolen the card and gone on a London shopping spree. The credit card company may block further transactions. A blocked credit/ATM card overseas is a travel hassle to avoid.

Traveler's Checks

Traveler's checks have become monetary dinosaurs, largely replaced by the plastic convenience of credit and ATM cards. For most travelers, there is no reason to buy traveler's checks or traveler's check cards.

Traveler's checks incur currency conversion fees, when issued, when cashed, or both. But for those who insist on taking traveler's checks on a trip, checks issued in British pounds can be used directly in London without having to cash and convert the checks into local currency.

Be aware that many London merchants don't accept traveler's checks, and there may be a fee to cash them at banks, post offices, or other locations in London. Almost no London merchants will accept traveler's checks issued in dollars or other nonlocal currencies, and if they do, the transaction will include fees, sometimes hidden in unfavorable currency exchange rates.

Exchange Rate Roulette

The values of world currencies fluctuate, so keep an eye on foreign exchange rates before traveling. If it looks as if the value of your home currency may decline by the time you take your trip, consider prepaying some trip costs, such as car rental, hotel, and rail tickets. On the other hand, if it appears that the value of your currency may go up, don't prepay trip costs. Another strategy is to ignore the currency markets and enjoy your trip. This is especially true after arriving in London; you have no control over the international monetary market, so why sweat it?

Dash Cash

After spending long hours on a plane, claiming luggage, clearing customs and immigration, and navigating an unfamiliar airport, the last thing many travelers want to do is search for a place to get British pounds. One way to avoid this hassle is to take a small amount of British currency on the trip—enough to buy a snack or cover a taxi ride. Some travel agencies and banks sell foreign currency, and currency can be purchased online. Keep in mind that this is an expensive way to obtain pounds compared with using the ATMs in London.

That Nasty VAT

Many Americans are used to paying sales tax when they shop and readily accept a 5 or 10 percent tax added to the ticketed price. It comes as a shock to learn that you're paying 20 percent in value-added tax (VAT) when you rent a hotel room, buy a gift, eat dinner, or rent a car in Britain. European, Canadian, and other visitors are familiar with the VAT, although their home country rates may differ.

Most quoted prices in Britain include the VAT. That's one reason some things look really expensive in London (the other reason is that many things *are* really expensive). Refunds of the VAT are possible on some purchases, but you have to spend a lot in one store, complete some paperwork, and go through an extra customs line at the airport when leaving Britain. If you go into a London store and make a sizable purchase, the store may help process the VAT refund paperwork. Be sure to ask if the store has a VAT refund procedure.

Unless you are a specially registered business traveler, you can't recover the VAT on hotels, meals, or car rental. For tourists, this part of the VAT is an unavoidable cost of traveling in the European Union.

Good luck. It takes some work to save money this way. Many people don't bother with it, especially if they're not buying a lot of merchandise.

Britspeak

England and America are two countries separated
by a common language.
—Attributed to George Bernard Shaw

For American visitors, one great thing about going to England is that the people speak our language. Well, not exactly. As many tourists have learned, there's no such thing as universal English. Many British words and phrases differ significantly from those used by Americans, Canadians, Australians, and other English-speakers. Then there's the issue of accents, even when words or phrases are the same.

Skip to the Loo

The wise parent of young children is always toilet aware. Families traveling to London should know from the start that "bathrooms" in Britain are rooms where you take a bath. If that's not what you're looking for, here are some of the British terms that do apply:

- Loo
- WC
- Lavatory
- Gents
- Ladies
- Nappy-changing room (for babies)
- Toilet (can't argue that)

Finding a public toilet is not too difficult in London. Our children described the public toilet fee as "20p to pee." Toilets are also available in larger restaurants, hotel lobbies, museums, and department stores. If you look respectable, usually no one objects if you use these facilities, and they are often cleaner than public toilets.

More Britspeak

We use the term *Britspeak* to refer to some of the obvious differences between American English and the language spoken by most of the inhabitants of London. Here are a few Britspeak definitions for US visitors:

> **What they *say*—What they *mean***
>
> Aubergine—Eggplant
>
> Bill—Check (at a restaurant)
>
> Biscuits—Cookies
>
> Bonnet—Car hood
>
> Boot—Car trunk
>
> Cash point—Automated teller machine (ATM)
>
> Chemist shop—Drugstore, pharmacy
>
> Chips—French fries
>
> Clotted cream—A thick, sweet cream used as a teatime spread for bread or scones
>
> Coach—Bus
>
> Crisps—Potato chips
>
> Cuppa—Cup of tea
>
> Devonshire cream—Almost the same as clotted cream
>
> En suite—Private bath (in a hotel room)
>
> First floor—Second floor
>
> Flat—Apartment
>
> Flat white—espresso with microfoam
>
> Football—Soccer
>
> Fortnight—Two weeks
>
> Give way—Yield

Ground floor—First floor

Iced lolly—Popsicle

Jelly—Jell-O

Lay-by—Roadside parking pull-off area

Licensed—Restaurant with a liquor license

Lift—Elevator

Lorry—Truck

Maize—Corn

Nappy—Diaper

Pasty—Pastry turnover filled with vegetables and/or meat

Petrol—Gasoline, *expensive* gasoline

Post-box—Mailbox

Pram—Baby carriage

Priority—Right-of-way

Pudding—Dessert

Pushchair—Baby stroller

Queue—Line at a store, theater, or bus stop. Standing in
    queues is a national pastime in Britain

Quid—A pound (£)

Roundabout—Traffic circle

Scheme—Plan or program ("scheme" does not have a
    negative connotation)

Scone—A pastry; a sweet biscuit on which you pile clotted
    cream and jam at teatime (only fattening if you think
    about it)

Serviette—Napkin

Sterling—British pounds, money

Subway—Pedestrian underpass tunnel

Surgery—A doctor's or dentist's office

Takeaway—Carryout food

Tube—Subway

Underground—Subway

Way out—Exit

Zebra crossing—Pedestrian crossing (except at the zoo)

Tick-Tock

Although the clock face of Big Ben shows the familiar twelve hours, Britain officially uses a twenty-four-hour time system. "Officially" does not mean "uniformly," and Londoners are as likely to say 3:00 p.m. as they are to say 1500. Deciphering morning hours is easy: 0800 is 8:00 a.m., 1000 is 10:00 a.m., and so forth. When confronted with unfamiliar afternoon times, just remember to subtract 1200. So 1500 minus 1200 equals 3:00 p.m.

Time to Leave

No matter how long and fascinating your visit to London is, eventually it will be time to leave. How do you know for sure? If you're a savvy tourist, one who tries to blend in with the local scene, it may be time to depart when other tourists ask you for directions. Standing on a footbridge in St. James's Park, we were approached by an American tourist (a person whose regional accent was unmistakable):

"What's that building over there?" he asked.
"Buckingham Palace," we replied.
"Oh REALLY?" he answered, gawking in surprise.

Yep, it is definitely time to leave when other tourists mistake you for a local!

Back in the United States after fifteen days in London, our family unloaded piles of dirty laundry and then sat down to our first meal since returning home. Our son remarked, "I can't believe it. Last night we were having dinner at a pub in London. Today we're back at our kitchen table." That, son, is the magic of overseas travel. And it's the reason why we'll go back.

Index

Page numbers in *italic* indicate illustrations or maps.

Credits

If not noted, quotations or photos are in the public domain.

Page 114: Photo © Manual Harlan/Shakespeare's Globe.

Page 117: From *When We Were Very Young* © 1952 by A. A. Milne.

Page 119: Photo © visitlondonimages/britainonview.

Page 136: *Harry Potter and the Philosopher's Stone* © 2004 by J. K. Rowling.

Page 137: Photo © The Zoological Society of London.

Page 142: From *When We Were Very Young* © 1952 by A. A. Milne.

Page 143: Photo © visitlondonimages/britainonview.

Page 144: Photo © visitlondonimages/britainonview/Pawel Libera.

Page 149: "The Thames" by M. M. Hutchinson, from *A Book of a Thousand Poems* (Random House/Wing Books, 1993).

Page 151: © National Maritime Museum.

Page 179: Photo by kind permission of Blenheim Palace.

Page 181: Photo © Mike Dodman under the Creative Commons Attribution-ShareAlike 2.0 license.

Page 187: Photo © Deb Hosey White.

Page 193: Photo is licensed under the Creative Commons Attribution-Share Alike 2.0 Generic license by mattbuck.

Page 207: Photo © Ritz Hotel London.

Page 222: "Food, Glorious Food" from *Oliver!*, lyrics by Lionel Bart.

Page 225: Photo © Ritz Hotel London.

Page 234: *Mary Poppins* ©1934 by P. L. Travers.

Page 236: Photo © VisitBritain/Flackley Ash Hotel.

Page 243: Photo courtesy Historic Royal Palaces.

Page 250: Photo is licensed under the Creative Commons Attribution-Share Alike 2.0 Generic license by Tatsuhiko Miyagawa from San Francisco, United States.

Page 254: "The Wombling Song" by Michael Batt, *Wombling Songs* (CBS Records, 1973).

Page 257: *A Bear Called Paddington* © 1958 by Michael Bond.

Page 259: Photo © visitlondonimages/britainonview.com/Sheradon Dublin.

Page 261: *A Bear Called Paddington* © 1958 by Michael Bond.

Page 262: Photo used under the terms of the GNU Free Documentation License, http://commons.wikimedia.org/wiki/File:London_Taxi_1.jpg.

Page 263: *Paddington Goes to Town* © 1968 by Michael Bond.

Page 265: Photo © visitlondonimages/britainonview.com/Sheradon Dublin.

Page 271: *Paddington Goes to Town* © 1968 by Michael Bond.

Page 272: Photo © William Warby, Creative Commons license.

Page 298: Photo © Laura K. White.

All maps are by Kim Rusch.

About the Authors

David Stewart White began his adventures in family travel as a child, when he lived in Paris and traveled throughout Europe. His travel articles have appeared in the *Washington Post*, the *Charlotte Observer*, *Examiner.com*, and *AAA World Magazine* and in numerous travel websites and online magazines.

Deb Hosey White is the author of the novels *Pink Slips and Parting Gifts* and *Magic Numbers—The Actuary's Diary*. With English ancestors on both sides of her family, Deb is a serious Anglophile and an avid traveler.

In addition to the fifth edition of *Let's Take the Kids to London*, David and Deb are coauthors of *Portugal: A Tale of Small Cities*. They also created *Beyond Downton Abbey* and *Travels Beyond Downtown*, a guidebook series exploring great houses with great stories.

Deb and Dave live and write in North Carolina, where they are partners in Scuppernong Books, an independent bookstore.